Cooking with Three Ingredients

Flavorful Food
Easy as 1, 2, 3

To Étoi & Dante

Andrew Schloss

A John Boswell Associates/King Hill Productions Book

Quill
An Imprint of HarperCollins*Publishers*

HarperCollins books may be purchased for educational, business, or sales promotional use. For information please write: Special Markets Department, HarperCollins Publishers Inc., 10 East 53rd Street, New York, NY 10022.

First Quill edition published 2003.

Design: Barbara Cohen Aronica
Index: Maro Riofrancos

The Library of Congress has catalogued the hardcover edition as follows:

Schloss, Andrew.
    Cooking with 3 ingredients / Andrew Schloss.
      p. cm.
    "A John Boswell Associates/King Hill Productions book."
    Includes index.
    ISBN 0-06-017375-0
    1. Quick and easy cookery. I. Title.
    TX833.5.S34 1996
    641.5'123—dc20   96-6771

ISBN 0-06-055501-7 (pbk.)

03 04 05 06 07 ❖/RRD 10 9 8 7 6 5 4 3 2 1

Contents

Introduction: A Trio of Delights

I have a happy confession to make: Writing this book has transformed me from a cooking-from-scratch stickler to a streamlining fanatic. Now instead of thinking what else I can add to a pan sauce or a marinade, I think, "How do I get more with less?" Do I really need tomatoes and bell peppers and jalapeños and cumin and cilantro in my vegetable chili, if a few spoonfuls of salsa will give me the same effect with a single ingredient? If ketchup contains tomatoes, onions, sugar, vinegar, and spices, do I really need any more seasonings in my sweet and sour pot roast? And if that same roast is going to flavor the broth with rich beefy juices, what is the use of the beef broth I usually add?

I have learned to make a great beef borscht from short ribs, sauerkraut, and V-8 juice; a killer cocktail spread from goat cheese, sun-dried tomatoes, and tapenade; and a stuffed and glazed holiday turkey with just a bird, a package of corn bread stuffing mix, and a couple cans of cranberry sauce.

You'll find many inventive recipes (Fresh Tuna Braised with Caramelized Onions, Thai Peanut Shrimp), as well as modernized renditions of old standards (Finger Lickin' Oven-Fried Chicken, Steak au Poivre). They stretch the notion of what a known ingredient can be (Caribbean Ginger Tomato Soup made from a can of condensed tomato soup, a can of coconut milk, and fresh ginger); and turn brand-new ingredients into old friends (an envelope of Thai Peanut Salad Dressing Mix metamorphoses into a great Hot and Sour Peanut Soup).

What has made this book so much fun to write is the new generation of high-quality prepared foods that now populate our markets. I've come to see them as allies not just in an emergency for a quick meal, but when cooking any number of tasty dishes. They've allowed me to develop recipes that were never dreamed of by the manufacturers of these products. Just as condensed milk, canned soup, and frozen vegetables changed the way Americans cooked dinner from the 1850s through the 1950s, jarred salsa, bean dip, and instant couscous are revolutionizing meals today.

I invite you to tour your local market. Thai red curry paste, preserved lemon pickle, and jalapeño Tabasco sauce share shelf space with the Worcestershire and ketchup. The soup aisle brims with hot and sour soup, dried bean blends, six different flavors of ramen noodles, and canned gazpacho. There is coconut milk, molasses mustard, and Cajun-style stewed tomatoes. You'll see jars of ginger puree and pesto next to salad dressings flavored with sun-dried tomatoes. Cheeses are studded with hot peppers and herbs. Even garlic is sold as a convenience item, already minced in oil.

All of the recipes in these pages call for just three ingredients (not counting salt, pepper, and water), and occasionally I've opted for prepared foods that in themselves contain more than three ingredients. In this regard my children have accused me of cheating. To their way of thinking the three-ingredient goulash we just had for dinner is an impostor. It's a case of simple mathematics. The onions are one ingredient, paprika is two, but the marinated London broil? Only our butcher knows for sure. I admit that the marinated steak from the meat case in my supermarket probably has more than a half-dozen ingredients in it, but so does the ketchup I put in barbecue sauce, or the chicken broth I add to soup. The fact that convenience ingredients are now as likely to come from the local butcher or deli or bakery as they are from a distant food conglomerate not only makes cooking from scratch easier, but it makes convenience recipes more exciting and that much closer to homemade.

Sorting out the quality products from the frauds can take some time.

My advice is to start with things you know and take some risks. If you know you like tomato salsa over your grilled chicken, speculate on a mango salsa, and if that works, try a mango chutney. In time maybe you'll be serving your own famous three-ingredient Tamarind Chicken Curry on a bed of Couscous. And you thought convenience foods were boring?

Here's a list of some of the more unusual ingredients that I've used in developing recipes for this book, along with a brief description of each, and some suggestions on how and where to find them.

Ingredients to Look For

Asian Sesame Oil This very fragrant oil is made from toasted sesame seeds and is sometimes called toasted sesame oil. It has a golden, deep amber color and is sold in the Asian section of supermarkets.

Basil Pesto Sauce This aromatic herb paste is best made fresh, but jarred and refrigerated versions are readily available.

Beans, Instant All you do is add water to these preseasoned dehydrated bean powders to transform them into amazingly good fat-free bean dips. These all-natural products are sold mostly in health food stores, but as the penchant for beans and bean products grows, they are showing up in more and more supermarkets. Usually promoted as a base for dips or refried beans, their potential as a soup base or sauce thickener cannot be overstated.

Black Bean Sauce with Garlic This Chinese sauce is made from fermented soy beans, just like soy sauce. It is thick and intense, and especially salty. Use it sparingly. You'll find it in the Asian food section of your supermarket and at Chinese markets.

Cajun Spices A salted hot pepper spice blend sold along with other seasonings in most markets.

Chiles, Dried There are hundreds of varieties of chile peppers. The only unusual varieties used in this book are chipotles, which are smoked jalapeños, and New Mexico chiles, called for as a ground powder. Chipotles can be bought dried or canned in adobo sauce. New Mexico chile powder is sold in specialty food shops.

Coconut Milk, Unsweetened   Sold canned alongside other Asian ingredients, coconut milk is sometimes available in a reduced-fat version, but in my testing it does not compare in quality to regular unsweetened coconut milk.

Dried Wild Mushrooms   There are many varieties of dried mushrooms sold in the produce or gourmet sections of markets. Some of the most common are porcini, morels, shiitakes, chanterelles, or a generic product usually called forest mushrooms. After soaking they are both meatier and more pungent than their fresh counterparts, which often makes them preferable in soups and sauces.

Garlic, Minced   Jarred garlic is sold packed in water or in oil, minced or coarsely chopped. The oil-based products have a more natural garlic flavor. Roasted or browned garlic is also available.

Ginger Preserves   This jam of chopped ginger and sugar is not to be confused with preserved ginger. Ginger preserves are a British product sold in the jelly aisle of your market. The brand I buy is Dundee, which is made in Australia.

Herb Cheese   There are many brands and varieties of cheeses that are flavored with herbs. When I call for herb cheese I'm referring to the soft, spreadable varieties. Most include garlic, basil, oregano, thyme, or dill. The nationally distributed brands are Rondele, Crème du Lait, and Boursin, which are all cream cheeses. In a few recipes chèvre, or goat cheese, is specified. Herb chèvre is available in any well-stocked cheese section of a market or in any cheese store.

Herbes de Provence   An herb blend sold in the seasoning section of most markets, it is a mix of herbs—typically basil, fennel seed, lavender, marjoram, rosemary, sage, savory, and thyme—that are native to the south of France.

Hoisin Sauce Made from fermented soy beans, just like soy sauce, hoisin is thicker and sweeter, and quite salty. It is available in the Asian section of your market.

Hot Pepper Sauce These days some supermarkets have entire sections devoted just to hot sauces, ranging from the familiar spicy Tabasco to fiery habeñero sauces. You'll note a number of recipes in this book that specify *mild* hot pepper sauce; several call for Durkee Red Hot Sauce by name. I do believe that particular brand is the only choice for anything cooked Buffalo style.

Jalapeño Tabasco Sauce Made from mild jalapeño peppers, this new green Tabasco product looks like it would be more fiery than the more familiar red sauce, but it is gentler, more aromatic, and sweeter.

Lemon Preserves This is a jam of chopped whole lemons and sugar, not to be confused with Indian pickled lemon or Moroccan preserved lemons wedges packed in salt. Lemon preserves is a British product, similar to a coarse marmalade. It is sold in the jelly aisle of your market. The brand I buy is Dundee, made in Australia.

Old Bay Seasoning A salty, spicy seasoning blend from the Chesapeake Bay that is most traditionally used for boiling crabs. It is sold in the seasoning section of your market in a large yellow tin.

Olives Black olives are ripe green olives. They have more flavor, are softer, and often less salty than their green counterparts. Most of the time that I call for olives, it will be black ripe olives. They can be any type— Niçoise, Mislinis, Kalamata—but do not use canned California olives. These ersatz black olives are not ripe and were never cured. They have none of the dark, earthy fermented flavors that ripe olives should provide and will not yield good results.

Olive Paste (Tapenade) This puree of oil-cured black olives, garlic, olive oil, and herbs is available in many gourmet groceries. It can be mail ordered from Dean & DeLuca, 560 Broadway, New York, NY 10012 (212) 431-1691.

Plum or Duck Sauce   This very sweet, fruity Chinese sauce, the condiment served with fried noodles at Chinese restaurants, has two names. Duck Sauce is orange in color and smooth. The same thing can be called Plum Sauce, which tastes.the same but is darker and chunkier. You will find both names in the Asian section of your market.

Ricotta Salata   This is aged, salted ricotta. It is firm enough to slice, fairly dry, and lightly tangy. As cheeses go, it is fairly low in fat. Feta makes an acceptable substitute.

Sun-Dried Tomatoes   As the name implies these are dried tomatoes, made in much the same way that raisins are made from grapes. They can be bought unadorned, packed in oil, or worked into a paste. All of the recipes in this book that use sun-dried tomatoes call for the oil-cured variety. These come jarred, or you can cure them yourself by rehydrating the unadorned sun-dried tomatoes in boiling water and then packing them in olive oil.

Teriyaki Sauce   A Japanese barbecue sauce made from soy sauce, sweeteners, and seasoning. Available in the Asian section of your market.

Thai Spicy Peanut Salad Dressing Mix   This envelope of powder can be mixed with water or coconut milk to make a robust, spicy hot sauce. It is available at Asian markets, at health food stores, or in the Asian section of your supermarket. Taste of Thai will sell it by mail order: P.O. Box AX, Old Saybrook, CT 06475 (203) 388-0838.

Thai Peanut Sauce   This bottled product is ready to use. It is somewhat salty, very fragrant, and has a healthy kick. It can be found in the Asian section of many supermarkets.

Tomato Paste in a Tube   The best tomato paste I have ever found is packed in a tube by an Italian company, Amore. It is very sweet, and best of all, the tube keeps any leftover paste fresh for months. No more throwing out half-used cans of fuzzy tomato paste.

Dips, Spreads, Appetizers, and Snacks

Herbed Spinach Dip

Lemon Honey Dip

Bagna Cauda

Green Olive Tapenade

Lemon Lovers' Hummus

Smoky Baba Ganouche

Goat Cheese Provençal

Chili Beany Nachos

Very Cheesy Nachos

Chickpea Poppers

Sweet-Heat Almonds

Figs with Prosciutto and Mint

Saga Blue Grapes

Baked Buffalo Wings

Peppery Blackened Peppers

Extra-Virgin Popcorn

Feta and Artichoke Pizza

Triple Garlic Cheese

Peachy Smoked Salmon Mousse

Shrimp Dijonnaise

Herbed Spinach Dip

Spinach lends an aura of nutrition to the explosion of flavor that is the essence of this dip. There are many varieties of garlic and herb cream cheese available now. Any will do; this recipe even works well with reduced-fat products.

1 ¹/₄ CUPS, ENOUGH FOR 4 TO 6 SERVINGS

- **1 box (10 ounces) frozen chopped spinach**
- **1 package (6 ounces) garlic and herb cream cheese**
- **2 tablespoons grated Parmesan cheese**

1   Defrost the spinach in its box in a microwave on high power for 4 minutes. Remove from the box and drain in a strainer, pushing out as much water as possible.

2   Combine the spinach, cream cheese, and Parmesan cheese in a food processor or blender. Puree until smooth. Season to taste with salt and pepper. Serve as a dip for vegetables or chips or as a spread for bread or crackers.

Lemon Honey Dip

Children are the most reactionary of eaters, but even the pickiest will lap up this subtly sweet, tangy dip. It can make even broccoli palatable.

ABOUT 1¼ CUPS, ENOUGH FOR 4 TO 6 SERVINGS

- **1 cup (8 ounces) plain yogurt**
- **Juice of ½ lemon**
- **1 tablespoon honey**

In a medium bowl, combine the yogurt, lemon juice, and honey. Mix to blend well. Season with a little salt to taste, if you feel it's needed. Serve as a dip with vegetables.

Bagna Cauda

This very simple, ancient Roman dip is served warm. It can be drizzled over boiled potatoes, smeared on bread, tossed with hot pasta, or drawn as a bath for fresh vegetables.

ABOUT ¾ CUP, ENOUGH FOR 4 TO 6 SERVINGS

- ½ cup extra-virgin olive oil
- 2 cloves garlic, minced
- 1 tin (2 ounces) flat anchovy fillets, drained and finely chopped

1 In a small saucepan, heat the olive oil with the garlic over low heat just until the garlic starts to release its aroma, about 2 minutes. Do not allow it to color at all.

2 Add the anchovies and continue to cook, stirring, until the anchovies dissolve into a rough paste, about 2 minutes.

3 Season with pepper to taste and serve while warm.

Green Olive Tapenade

Tapenade, the rich olive sauce of Provence, is usually made from ripe black olives. This rendition gives tradition a tweak by substituting leaner, saltier green olives. It is just right spread on toasts to serve with drinks, but it is equally good served as a cold sauce for grilled chicken or fish, or as a dip for vegetables.

ABOUT 1 CUP, ENOUGH FOR 4 SERVINGS

- **1 cup pitted small green olives**
- **2 cloves garlic, crushed or minced**
- **¼ cup extra-virgin olive oil**

In a blender or food processor, or with a large knife by hand, finely chop the olives and garlic. Blend in the olive oil to make a paste. Season to taste with salt and pepper.

Lemon Lovers' Hummus

Hummus, the ubiquitous Middle Eastern chickpea puree, is normally enriched with olive oil. This one replaces the oil with water, making a lower-fat alternative for spreading on pita, tortillas, or bagels. It is a natural dip for vegetables and chips, and a great sauce for sandwiches. The traditional lemony flavor of hummus is heightened here by using both the zest, the colored part of the peel, and the juice of a lemon.

1 3/4 CUPS, ENOUGH FOR 6 SERVINGS

- **1 lemon**
- **2 cups (15-ounce can) cooked chickpeas, drained**
- **2 cloves garlic, coarsely chopped**

1 Remove the zest from the lemon with a fine-tooth grater or a zester. If removed with a zester, chop finely.

2 Squeeze the juice from the lemon into a food processor or blender. Add the lemon zest, chickpeas, garlic, and 2 tablespoons water.

3 Puree until smooth. Season to taste with salt and pepper.

Smoky Baba Ganouche

The deep, smoky redolence of this eggplant spread does not come from a particular ingredient—it radiates from the preparation. Instead of being sautéed or baked, the eggplant is charred over a flame. As the surface blackens, the inside steams and is permeated by smoke from the burning skin. This is a great dip for chips and vegetables, a wonderful spread, and an interesting addition to meaty soups, stews, and gravies.

ABOUT 1¹/₂ CUPS, ENOUGH FOR 6 SERVINGS

- **1 medium eggplant**
- **2 cloves garlic, minced**
- **2 tablespoons bottled balsamic vinaigrette**

1 Poke the eggplant with the tines of a fork in several places. Place directly over the flame of a grill, a gas burner, or under a broiler. Cook until the skin chars, turning it with tongs every 3 to 4 minutes to blacken the skin uniformly. When the eggplant is charred all over, it will be soft inside.

2 As soon as the eggplant is cool enough to handle, cut off the stem cap and split the eggplant in half lengthwise. With a large spoon, scrape the eggplant into a food processor or blender. Discard the blackened skin.

3 Add the garlic and vinaigrette. Puree until smooth. Season to taste with salt and pepper.

Goat Cheese Provençal

This spread assembles the flavors of Provence into a pungent, salty, sweet, and fragrant cheese. It is great on bread, especially a crusty sourdough or an herbed French bread. It's not bad melted over pasta, either.

ABOUT 1¼ CUPS, ENOUGH FOR 6 SERVINGS

- **1 package (5½ ounces) fresh goat cheese (chèvre)**
- **8 to 10 (depending on size) sun-dried tomatoes in oil, coarsely chopped, plus 2 teaspoons oil from jar**
- **2 teaspoons black olive paste**

In a food processor or blender, combine the goat cheese, dried tomatoes, oil from the tomatoes, and the olive paste. Puree until smooth. Season to taste with pepper.

Chili Beany Nachos

Nachos are an addictive snack. And since it is impossible to not finish the plate once you've started, this recipe ensures that you will at least get a modicum of nutrition with your indulgences. The beans and chips are complementary proteins, and you can lower the fat by using baked tortilla chips and reduced-fat cheese.

4 SERVINGS

1 can (15 ounces) chili beans

6 cups (4½ ounces) tortilla chips

4 ounces jalapeño Monterey Jack cheese, shredded

1 In a small saucepan, warm the beans over medium heat, stirring, until heated through, about 3 minutes.

2 Pile the tortilla chips on a large dinner plate. Spoon the beans over the chips and scatter the cheese over the top.

3 Microwave on high power for 1 minute (or bake at 375°F for 3 to 4 minutes), until the cheese melts.

Very Cheesy Nachos

Cheese is the main attraction of these nachos. It's doubled by stacking the ingredients and cooking them in layers.

4 SERVINGS

- **6 cups (4½ ounces) tortilla chips**
- **8 ounces Cheddar or Monterey Jack cheese, shredded**
- **1 cup chunky salsa (hot or medium)**

1 Pile half the chips on a large dinner plate. Top with half the cheese. Microwave on high power for 1 minute (or bake at 375°F about 3 to 4 minutes), until the cheese melts.

2 Spoon the salsa over the top. Cover with the remaining chips and the remaining cheese. Return to the microwave or oven and cook again for the same amount of time. Serve at once.

Chickpea Poppers

Sautéed chili-glazed chickpeas, otherwise known as garbanzo beans, are a lot like spiced nuts—you keep popping them in your mouth. And the beans contain a fraction of the fat. These can be made ahead and kept at room temperature for a day before serving.

4 TO 6 SERVINGS

2 cups (15-ounce can) cooked chickpeas, drained

2 tablespoons Asian sesame oil

2 tablespoons chili powder

1 Heat a nonstick skillet over medium-high heat for 1 minute. Add the chickpeas and cook for 1 to 2 minutes, stirring constantly, until the chickpeas are dry and lightly toasted. Reduce the heat to medium.

2 Add the sesame oil, chili powder, and a few good shakes of salt. Cook and stir until the chickpeas are coated with oil and spices, about 1 minute.

Sweet-Heat Almonds

These sugar-glazed, hot-lipped little scorchers are amazingly addictive. Store them at room temperature, but keep them away from moisture and humidity, which can cause the glaze to soften.

4 SERVINGS

- **1 cup whole almonds in their skins**
- **¼ cup sugar**
- **¼ teaspoon cayenne**

1　Heat a nonstick skillet over high heat for 1 minute. Add the almonds and reduce the heat to medium-low. Cook, stirring, until the almonds are lightly toasted, 3 to 4 minutes.

2　Add the sugar and keep stirring until the sugar melts and browns, about 30 seconds. (*Be careful: Caramelized sugar can give a nasty burn.*) Immediately turn out the nuts onto a sheet pan and sprinkle with the cayenne and plenty of salt.

3　Wait for a minute or two, until the almonds are just cool enough to touch. Break them into individual almonds. Do not wait too long, or the sugar will harden and it will be difficult to separate the nuts.

Figs with Prosciutto and Mint

The combination of sweet juicy fruit and dry salt-cured ham is an attraction of opposites. An antipasto of melon and prosciutto is a classic of the genre. Here, fresh figs replace the melon, but it is the mentholated addition of mint that makes these morsels so special.

4 APPETIZER SERVINGS

- **6 ripe fresh figs**
- **3 paper-thin slices of imported prosciutto (prosciutto di Parma)**
- **12 small mint sprigs**

1 Cut the tip off the stem of each fig. Cut each fig in half lengthwise. Cut each slice of prosciutto lengthwise into 4 strips.

2 Place a mint sprig on the cut side of each fig and wrap a strip of prosciutto around each piece, securing the mint sprig in place, but allowing some of the green to show.

Saga Blue Grapes

Fruit, nuts, and cheese combine here in compact pop-in-your-mouth morsels. You can make these ahead and store them tightly wrapped in the refrigerator, but plan to serve within 24 hours.

4 TO 6 APPETIZER SERVINGS

- **½ pound walnuts, finely chopped**
- **10 ounces Saga Blue cheese, rind removed**
- **24 large seedless grapes (red or green)**

1 Heat a nonstick skillet over high heat for 1 minute. Reduce the heat to low. Add the walnuts and cook, stirring, until the nuts are lightly toasted, 2 to 3 minutes. Transfer to a shallow bowl and set aside to cool.

2 In a small bowl, beat the cheese until soft. Season with salt and pepper to taste.

3 With wet hands, mold the cheese around the grapes and roll in the toasted nuts to coat. Arrange like a bunch of grapes on a serving platter.

Baked Buffalo Wings

Legend has it that Teresa Bellisimo, owner of the Anchor Bar in Buffalo, New York, was delivered an excess of chicken wings in the winter of 1964 and decided to serve them in a glaze of hot sauce. Buffalo Chicken Wings were an instant success, and they put this city in northwestern New York on the map. So great was their impact that in 1977, the city of Buffalo declared July 29 "Chicken Wing Day."

4 SERVINGS

- **24 chicken wings (about 4 pounds)**
- **6 tablespoons butter, melted**
- **3 tablespoons Durkee Red Hot Sauce**

1 Preheat oven to 450°F. Cut the chicken wings into 3 sections, discarding the tip section or saving it for making broth.

2 Toss the remaining wing sections with 1 tablespoon of the butter. Arrange the wings in a single layer in a 9-by-13-inch baking pan and bake until crisp, about 45 minutes.

3 Melt the remaining butter in a small saucepan over medium-low heat and stir in the hot sauce. Toss with the fully cooked wings and serve.

Peppery Blackened Peppers

Roasted peppers are a miraculous creation: fat-free, full of vitamin C, and able to turn anything they touch instantly gourmet. The roasting is easy, and as convenient to do with a dozen peppers as it is with one or two. Place directly over the high flame of a gas burner or grill. If you only have electric cooking surfaces, split the peppers in half lengthwise and broil skin-side up. Roasted peppers can be stored in the refrigerator, lightly coated with oil, for up to 10 days. I like to have some on hand to offer as an instant appetizer on slices of crusty bread.

4 SERVINGS

3 red, yellow, or orange bell peppers

1 teaspoon minced garlic in oil

¾ teaspoon coarsely ground black pepper

1   Roast the peppers directly over a high flame. Turn so that the skins of the peppers blacken evenly. When completely charred, place the peppers in a paper bag, close loosely, and set aside for 10 minutes.

2   Peel the roasted peppers with your fingers. The skin will slip off easily. If it clings to your fingers, wash them off and continue peeling, but avoid running the peppers under water, for it will wash away much of their flavor. Remove the stems and seeds and cut the peppers into wide strips.

3   Toss the roasted pepper strips with the minced garlic, coarsely ground pepper, and salt to taste.

Extra-Virgin Popcorn

Buttered popcorn, watch out. Nothing beats a little garlic and a bath of a full-bodied, aromatic virgin olive oil

4 LARGE SERVINGS

- **¼ cup extra-virgin olive oil**
- **1 cup popping corn**
- **½ teaspoon garlic powder**

1   In a large heavy pot, heat 2 tablespoons of the olive oil over high heat until it smokes, about 2 minutes.

2   Add 1 kernel of popcorn as a test and heat until it pops. Add the remaining popcorn and cover the pot. Shake gently until the kernels start to pop, then shake more vigorously until the popping subsides. Every so often, crack the lid to allow steam to escape, but not so far as to let flying kernels out.

3   When the popping subsides, remove the pan from the heat. Toss the popcorn in a large bowl with the remaining olive oil, the garlic powder, and salt to taste.

Feta and Artichoke Pizza

The mass availability of prebaked pizza bread shells has changed the notion of homemade pizza. Although not quite the same as fresh-baked varieties, they are ready in 10 minutes and are a delicious cross between pizza and an open-faced submarine sandwich. This one is topped effortlessly and flavorfully with jarred marinated artichoke hearts and an avalanche of crumbled feta cheese.

4 PORTIONS

1 jar (12 ounces) marinated artichoke hearts, marinade reserved

7 ounces feta cheese, crumbled

1 large (12-inch) prebaked Italian bread shell, such as Boboli

1 Preheat oven to 400°F. Cut the artichoke hearts into quarters and mix with the feta and ¼ cup of the marinade from the artichokes.

2 Spread over the top of the bread shell and bake for 10 minutes, or until the cheese is melted.

3 Let the pizza rest for 3 minutes. Cut into wedges and serve.

Triple Garlic Cheese

Seasoned cream cheeses are easy to make yourself. This garlicky one is a low-fat version using farmer cheese, a dry-curd cream cheese. If farmer cheese is unavailable in your area, substitute reduced-fat cream cheese, often called Neufchâtel. Serve as a spread with crackers or bread.

1 CUP, ENOUGH FOR 4 TO 6 PORTIONS

- **8 ounces farmer cheese**
- **1 teaspoon balsamic vinegar**
- **3 cloves garlic, minced**

1 In a small bowl, combine the cheese, vinegar, and garlic. Mix to blend well. Season liberally with salt and pepper.

2 Wet your hands and form the cheese into a dome on a small plate. Dust with more pepper, if desired.

Peachy Smoked Salmon Mousse

Salt and sweet don't cancel each other out. They jar and spar and spark the taste buds into doing excited topsy-turvy back flips. Here the saltiness of smoked salmon is dispersed in a balm of cream cheese and piped into perfectly ripe peaches. The peach is presented sitting straight up, with a rosette of the mousse peeking from its core. (If you have them, mint sprigs make a lovely optional garnish.) The colors are subtle, the presentation is arresting, and the surprising combination of flavors ceases to be strange the minute you take a bite.

4 SERVINGS

- **6 ounces cream cheese, softened**
- **2 ounces smoked salmon, cut into small pieces**
- **4 ripe peaches, preferably Freestone**

1 In a food processor, combine the cream cheese and the salmon. Puree until smooth. Set the smoked salmon mousse aside.

2 Cut a thin slice from the bottom of each peach, so it will stand upright. Insert a small spoon (a grapefruit spoon works well) into the top of each peach on one side of the stem. Slide it down the side of the pit and wiggle it gently. Do the same thing down the other side of the pit. The pit will now be free and you can lift it out with the spoon.

3 Pipe or spoon the smoked salmon mousse into the cavity in the peach, mounding slightly out of the top.

Shrimp Dijonnaise

This makes an elegant appetizer or hors d'oeuvre. If serving the shrimp as a pickup, remove them from their marinade and serve on toothpicks. For a sit-down appetizer, arrange them on a plate and nap with the sauce.

4 SERVINGS

- **1 pound large (26 to 30 count) shrimp, peeled and deveined**
- **½ cup ranch dressing**
- **¼ cup whole-grain Dijon mustard**

1 In a small saucepan, heat 1 cup water to a boil over high heat. Season to taste with salt and pepper and add the shrimp. Stir until all of the shrimp have been exposed to the water. Cover and remove from the heat. Set aside for 1 minute.

2 Meanwhile, in a serving bowl, mix the ranch dressing with the mustard. Season to taste with salt and pepper.

3 Drain the shrimp well and mix with the sauce while they are still hot. Refrigerate for 1 hour before serving. Toss once or twice while they are marinating, if you have the time.

Soups, Chowders, Broths, and Bisques

Garlic Penicillin

Lemon Chicken Soup

Beany Corn Soup

Bacon Bean Soup

Chunky Corn Chowder with Spicy Sausage

Cream of Tomato-Basil Soup

Caribbean Ginger Tomato Soup

Cheddar Tomato Soup

Sweet and Sour Beef Borscht

Popeye's Mushroom Soup (without Olive Oyl)

Sweet Onion Soup

No-Cook Beet Borscht

Limey Scallop Soup

Hot and Sour Peanut Soup

Harvest Squash Soup

Potato Leek Soup

Broccoli Tarragon Bisque

Garlic Penicillin

This is a magical soup. I don't know if it's the power of chicken broth, the garlic, or the vitamin C in the lemon, but together they seem to stop any ailment right in its tracks. It is the perfect soup for sipping from a mug.

4 SERVINGS

4 cups chicken broth

1 teaspoon minced garlic

Juice of ½ lemon

1 Combine the broth and garlic in a medium saucepan. Bring to a simmer over medium heat.

2 Remove the broth from the heat and stir in the lemon juice.

3 Season with salt and pepper to taste. Serve while piping hot.

Lemon Chicken Soup

Traditional *avgolemono,* a lemony chicken soup from Greece, is enriched with egg. Here the egg has been deleted, making a lighter, more versatile broth. This version has the comfort of chicken and rice, with a bracing burst of lemon. It serves well as a first course before roasted poultry, or as a light lunch with salad and bread.

4 SERVINGS

- **4 cups chicken broth**
- **⅓ cup long-grain white rice**
- **1 lemon**

1 In a heavy medium saucepan, combine the broth with ⅔ cup water. Bring to a boil over medium-high heat. Add the rice, stir, cover, and cook until the rice is tender, about 12 minutes.

2 Meanwhile, grate the zest from the lemon. Add to the soup and simmer 3 to 5 minutes longer. Season to taste with salt and pepper.

3 Remove from the heat. Stir in the lemon juice and serve at once.

Bean Soups

The following two soups get their depth of flavor from instant powdered dried beans. These all-natural, fat-free products are sold mostly through health food stores, but as the penchant for beans and bean products grows, I have begun to see them in more and more supermarkets. Usually promoted as a base for bean dips or refried beans, their potential as a soup base is phenomenal.

Both of the following soups are hearty enough for a main course, and become a complete protein when accompanied by corn muffins or whole grain bread.

Beany Corn Soup

4 SERVINGS

- **1 box (7 ounces) instant refried beans**
- **1 can (11 ounces) Mexican-style corn**
- **1 cup chunky salsa (hot or medium)**

1   In a large saucepan, bring 4 cups water to a boil. Stir in the instant refried beans and corn. Bring to a simmer and cook over medium heat for 3 minutes, stirring often.

2   Stir in the salsa. Season to taste with salt and pepper. Serve hot.

Bacon Bean Soup

4 SERVINGS

5 strips of bacon, chopped

1 box (7 ounces) instant black beans or instant refried beans

1 can (15½ ounces) black or red kidney beans, drained and rinsed

1 In a large heavy saucepan, cook the bacon over medium heat until crisp, 4 to 5 minutes.

2 Remove from the heat. Add the instant black beans or refried beans and 4 cups water. Stir in the canned beans. Bring to a simmer and cook over medium heat for 3 minutes, stirring often. Season to taste with salt and pepper. Serve hot.

Chunky Corn Chowder with Spicy Sausage

This hearty chowder makes a great supper any time of the year. I serve it with fresh sliced tomatoes and warm tortillas in summer, or macaroni and cheese and a big slice of crusty black bread when the weather turns chilly.

4 SERVINGS

¼ pound (4 ounces) hot Italian sausage, casing removed, broken up

1 can (11 ounces) Mexican-style corn

3 cups chicken broth

1 In a large heavy saucepan, cook the sausage over medium heat, stirring occasionally, until the sausage loses its raw look and has been separated uniformly into small bits, 3 to 5 minutes.

2 Add the corn and broth. Simmer for 5 minutes.

3 Season to taste with salt and pepper. Serve hot.

Cream of Tomato-Basil Soup

If the Campbell's Soup Company had been started by Italian immigrants rather than by Scots, this is what the first canned soup might have been: homespun American cream of tomato goes Mediterranean. It's amazing what a little fresh basil can do.

3 TO 4 SERVINGS

- **1 can (10¾ ounces) condensed tomato soup**
- **1½ cups milk**
- **¼ cup finely chopped fresh basil leaves**

1 In a heavy medium saucepan, mix together all of the ingredients. Bring to a boil over medium heat, stirring often.

2 Season to taste with salt and pepper. Serve at once.

Caribbean Ginger Tomato Soup

Don't let this unusual combination of ingredients scare you. Their integration is alchemistic. You'd never guess this soup came out of cans.

3 TO 4 SERVINGS

1 can (10¾ ounces) condensed tomato soup

1½ cups canned unsweetened coconut milk

1 tablespoon grated fresh ginger

1   In a heavy medium saucepan, mix together all of the ingredients. Bring to a boil over medium heat, stirring often.

2   Season to taste with salt and pepper. Serve hot.

Cheddar Tomato Soup

Cheddar and tomato are a classic combo. There's grilled cheese and tomato, and tomato soup with grilled cheese, but this is the only time you'll see the two in the same bowl. The Cheddar gives the tomato richness and depth of flavor; the tomato reciprocates with the sweetness of fresh fruit. It's a great soup for a heartwarming lunch on a cold day or for a light supper with toast.

3 TO 4 SERVINGS

1 can (10¾ ounces) condensed tomato soup

¾ cup milk

8 ounces shredded sharp Cheddar cheese (about 2 cups)

1   In a heavy saucepan, mix together the soup and milk. Stir in ½ can of water and a generous shake of pepper. Bring to a simmer over medium heat.

2   Reduce the heat to low and whisk in the cheese just until melted. Do not overcook, or the cheese will separate.

Sweet and Sour Beef Borscht

A very hearty main course soup full of rich beefy flavors, the tang of sauerkraut, and the sweetness of garden vegetables. Make it a day ahead; it gets better with age. Top with a dollop of sour cream if you like and serve with slices of very fresh rye bread.

4 SERVINGS

1½ pounds beef short ribs

1 pound sauerkraut, drained

2 cups vegetable cocktail juice

1 Season the short ribs with salt and pepper. Set them over a hot fire on a grill or 4 inches from the heat of a broiler and cook, turning until nicely browned all over, 8 to 10 minutes.

2 Rinse the sauerkraut in a bowl of cold water and drain. Place in a large, heavy nonreactive saucepan. Add the short ribs, vegetable juice, and 3 cups water. Bring to a boil over medium heat. Reduce the heat to low, cover, and simmer until the meat is tender, about 1 hour.

3 Remove the short ribs from the soup. Cut the meat from the bones and cut into small dice. Return the meat to the soup; discard the bones. Season the soup with salt and pepper to taste. Thin with more water, if needed.

Popeye's Mushroom Soup (without Olive Oyl)

Is there a cupboard in America that doesn't have a can of condensed cream of mushroom soup on one of its shelves? It has been the inspiration for countless quick meals, and this is another. The easiest way to thaw frozen spinach is in the microwave. Do it right in the box at full power for 4 minutes.

4 SERVINGS

- **1 can (10¾ ounces) condensed cream of mushroom soup**
- **1 teaspoon minced garlic**
- **1 box (10 ounces) frozen chopped spinach, thawed**

1 In a large nonreactive saucepan, combine the soup with 2 cups water and the garlic. Bring to a boil over medium heat, stirring often.

2 Squeeze as much moisture as possible from the spinach. Stir into the soup and cook 1 minute longer. Season to taste with salt and pepper before serving.

Sweet Onion Soup

The flavor of this soup comes from sweet, mild Vidalia onions. If you can't find them or they are out of season, you can substitute another sweet onion, like Maui, Spanish, or Bermuda. This soup is at home served opulently before a roast, or casually alongside an omelet. For a one-pot meal, ladle the onion soup into heatproof bowls, top each with a piece of toasted French bread, pile it with grated Gruyère cheese, and run the whole thing under a broiler until the cheese cascades across the surface of the soup.

4 SERVINGS

3 tablespoons unsalted butter

1 large Vidalia onion, cut into eighths and thinly sliced

1 packet (1⅓ ounces) dry onion soup mix

1 In a heavy medium saucepan over medium-low heat, melt the butter. Add the onion and cook, stirring often, until the onion is very soft and just beginning to color, about 15 minutes.

2 Add 3 cups water and the onion soup mix and stir to combine. Raise the heat to medium-high and bring to a simmer. Simmer for 5 minutes. Season to taste with salt and pepper.

No-Cook Beet Borscht

Not everyone likes beets. I adore them, so I am probably not a fair judge of this soup. It is one of my favorites. As far as I'm concerned, there is nothing better at the end of a scorching summer day. And there's nothing easier or faster when it's too hot to go into the kitchen. Serve it with deli sandwiches.

4 SERVINGS

- **1 jar (16 ounces) pickled beets**
- **2 cups buttermilk**
- **⅓ cup chopped fresh dill**

1 Empty the jar of beets with its liquid into a food processor or blender. Pulse to chop finely.

2 Transfer the chopped beets with their liquid to a serving bowl. Stir in the buttermilk, dill, and 1 cup ice cold water. Season to taste with salt and pepper. Refrigerate until chilled, if desired.

Limey Scallop Soup

The scallops are "cooked" in two ways in this novel soup. First they are lightly cured in lime juice, and then they are heated through by the warmth of hot broth. They can never overcook or get tough because they're never exposed to a fire.

4 SERVINGS

- **½ pound sea scallops**
- **Juice of 1 large lime**
- **4 cups chicken broth**

1 Rinse the scallops and remove the rigid muscle from the side of each scallop; some may already have this removed. Thinly slice the scallops horizontally.

2 Place the thinly sliced scallops in a heatproof serving bowl or small tureen. Sprinkle the lime juice over the scallops and toss to coat.

3 In a small saucepan, bring the chicken broth to a boil. Season to taste with salt and pepper and pour over the scallops. Stir well and serve.

Hot and Sour Peanut Soup

Peanut soup is a staple in African, Southeast Asian, and southern American cooking. All of the renditions are unique and usually complicated to prepare. This recipe is of the Southeast Asian variety, and its procedure has been simplified by the use of Thai peanut dressing. The stuff is quite spicy and quite addictive. It is one of several high-quality Thai ingredients produced and marketed by A Taste of Thai brand foods, which are distributed nationwide.

4 SERVINGS

- ½ cup basmati or jasmine rice
- 3 cups chicken broth
- 1 package (2.9 ounces) Thai Spicy Peanut Salad Dressing Mix

1 In a large heavy saucepan, combine the rice with 1 cup water. Bring to a boil, reduce the heat to low, cover, and simmer until the rice is tender, about 15 minutes.

2 Remove from the heat. Add the chicken broth and the peanut dressing mix. Stir to combine. Return to medium-high heat and simmer for 4 to 5 minutes. Stir and serve.

Harvest Squash Soup

This unusual soup makes a great first course for an autumnal feast or the main attraction of a midwinter supper. Serve it with a fall fruit salad and bran muffins.

3 TO 4 SERVINGS

- **1 can (16 ounces) solid-pack pumpkin**
- **1 packet (1⅓ ounces) dry onion soup mix**
- **2 tablespoons ginger preserves, chopped**

1   In a heavy medium saucepan, mix the pumpkin and onion soup with 3 cups water. Bring to a simmer over medium heat, stirring often. Simmer for 5 minutes.

2   Stir in the ginger preserves, season to taste with salt and pepper, and serve.

Potato Leek Soup

Potato soup is heartwarming, homey, sophisticated, and urbane. It is anything you want it to be, for any occasion, at any time. Serve it piping hot for a simple supper or garnished with chives and whipped cream at an elegant dinner party; then thin the leftovers with chilled buttermilk and serve it icy cold for the best lunch I know.

4 SERVINGS

- **3 medium leeks, white and tender green parts**
- **4 cups chicken broth**
- **1¼ pounds potatoes (any type), peeled and diced**

1 Slice the leeks thinly and rinse well in a large bowl of cold water. Lift them out of the water and place the wet leeks in a heavy pot. Cook over medium heat until the leeks soften, about 10 minutes, stirring occasionally.

2 Add the chicken broth and season with salt and pepper to taste. Cook 10 minutes longer.

3 Add the potatoes and cook until they are tender, about 15 minutes. Mash some of the potatoes with a vegetable masher or a large spoon to thicken the soup. Season to taste with more salt and pepper and serve.

Broccoli Tarragon Bisque

Ignore the name and don't tell anyone what's in this soup. Try as they might, they will never be able to guess. The sweetness of the tarragon blends seamlessly with the acrid cabbage flavor of broccoli, creating a third titillating sensation that's completely magical. Serve this soup as a first course before a grilled fish, a roasted chicken, or a cheese soufflé.

4 SERVINGS

- **1 bunch of broccoli**
- **2 large branches fresh tarragon or 1 teaspoon dried**
- **4 cups chicken broth**

1 With a small sharp knife, cut the ends off the broccoli stalks and peel the stalks. Cut the broccoli stalks and florets into thin slices.

2 Combine all the ingredients in a large heavy saucepan. Cook over medium heat until the broccoli is very tender, about 15 minutes.

3 With a slotted spoon, transfer the broccoli to a food processor or blender. Puree as smooth as possible. Mix in the remaining liquid. Season to taste with salt and pepper. Serve hot.

One, Two, Three Chicken Magic

Peking Chicken

Lemon-Garlic Chicken

Spiked Apple-Glazed Chicken

Sweet Ginger Chicken

Chicken à l'Orange

Finger-Lickin' Oven-Fried Chicken

Baked Hot Lips Jalapeño Chicken

Crispy Pecan-Crusted Chicken

Baked Chicken with Molasses-Mustard Glaze

Smoky Hot Pepper Chicken

Chicken Slathered in Roasted Garlic

Mahogany Chicken Wings

Broiled Hot Pepper Honey Hens

Grilled Chicken Breasts with Roasted Pepper Relish

Grilled Chicken Breasts with Artichoke Salsa

Peking Chicken

I love Peking Duck. Even without the pancakes and scallions, the sticky crackling sweetness of the skin slathered with salty, pungent hoisin sauce is unabashedly sensual. I've borrowed the same flavors for this chicken recipe, which doesn't require the multistep cooking process needed for duck.

4 SERVINGS

- **1 (4-pound) chicken, rinsed and dried, with giblets removed**
- **½ cup honey**
- **3 tablespoons hoisin sauce**

1 Preheat the oven to 450°F. Carefully loosen the skin of the chicken by running your fingers under the skin of the breast and legs, separating it gently from the meat underneath without tearing it. Rub the breast and leg meat underneath the skin with salt and pepper and season the inside cavity of the chicken liberally with salt and pepper.

2 Place the chicken, breast-side down, on a rack set above a rimmed sheet pan or baking dish and roast in the preheated oven for 20 minutes.

3 Meanwhile, mix the honey with the hoisin sauce. After the chicken has been in the oven 20 minutes, brush a thin film of this mixture over the bottom of the chicken and roast for 10 minutes longer. Turn the chicken breast-side up. Brush with the honey mixture. Roast for another 30 minutes, basting with more honey mixture every 5 minutes, until it has all been used. Carve and serve.

Lemon-Garlic Chicken

This recipe squeezes the last smidgen of flavor from its lemon. Lemon zest and garlic are slathered under the chicken skin, the juice is showered over the top halfway through the roasting, and the lemon shell is stuffed inside the bird where it continues to release its perfume in the heat of the oven.

4 SERVINGS

1 lemon

3 tablespoons minced garlic in oil

1 (4-pound) chicken, rinsed and dried, with giblets removed

1   Preheat the oven to 450°F. Remove the zest from the lemon with a fine-tooth grater or a zester. If removed with a zester, chop finely. Squeeze the juice from the lemon into a small cup. Mix in the lemon zest, garlic, and about ½ teaspoon each salt and pepper.

2   Season the cavity of the chicken liberally with salt and pepper. Carefully loosen the skin of the chicken by running your fingers under the skin of the breast and legs, separating it gently from the meat underneath without tearing it. Rub half the garlic mixture over the breast and leg meat of the chicken underneath the skin. Rub the remaining garlic mixture all over the outside of the chicken.

3   Place the chicken, breast-side down, on a rack set above a rimmed sheet pan or baking dish and roast for 20 minutes.

4   Turn the chicken breast-side up. Pour the lemon juice over the chicken. Place the lemon halves inside the chicken. Roast 30 to 35 minutes longer, basting with pan juices during the last 10 minutes, until the thigh juices run clear. Allow to rest for 5 minutes before carving.

Spiked Apple-Glazed Chicken

Apple juice concentrate delivers a wallop of flavor and enough natural sugars to create a beautiful glaze on the surface of a roast chicken. In this recipe, its flavors are magnified by a hint of brandy.

4 SERVINGS

- **½ cup frozen apple juice concentrate**
- **2 tablespoons brandy**
- **1 (4-pound) chicken, rinsed and dried, with giblets removed**

1 Preheat the oven to 450°F. In a small bowl, mix the apple juice concentrate with the brandy. Set the apple glaze aside.

2 Season the cavity of the chicken liberally with salt and pepper. Carefully loosen the skin of the chicken by running your fingers under the skin of the breast and legs, separating it gently from the meat underneath without tearing it. Spoon half the apple glaze under the skin of the breast and legs.

3 Place the chicken, breast side down, on a rack set above a rimmed sheet pan or baking dish and roast for 15 minutes. Brush some of the remaining apple glaze over the outside of the chicken and roast for 10 minutes longer.

4 Turn the chicken breast-side up. Roast for another 30 to 35 minutes, until the thigh juices run clear, basting with more of the apple glaze every 5 minutes, until it has all been used. Allow to rest for 5 minutes before carving. Skim the fat from the pan juices and spoon the pan juices over the chicken.

Sweet Ginger Chicken

Ginger preserves, a jamlike product, shouldn't be confused with preserved ginger, which is sugar-coated ginger slices. Ginger preserves are popular in Britain and are available here under several British and Australian labels. The brand sold in my locality is Dundee.

4 SERVINGS

- ⅓ cup ginger preserves
- 2 tablespoons teriyaki sauce
- 1 (4-pound) chicken, rinsed and dried, with giblets removed

1 Preheat the oven to 450°F. In a small bowl, mix the ginger preserves with the teriyaki sauce. Set the ginger glaze aside.

2 Season the cavity of the chicken liberally with salt and pepper. Carefully loosen the skin of the chicken by running your fingers under the skin of the breast and legs, separating it gently from the meat underneath without tearing it. Spoon half the ginger glaze under the skin of the breast and legs.

3 Place the chicken, breast-side down, on a rack set above a rimmed sheet pan or baking dish and roast for 15 minutes. Brush the outside of the chicken with some of the ginger glaze and roast for 10 minutes longer.

4 Turn the chicken breast-side up. Roast for another 30 to 35 minutes, until the thigh juices run clear, basting with more of the ginger glaze every 7 minutes, until it has all been used. Allow to rest for 5 minutes before carving.

Chicken à l'Orange

Chicken or duck à l'orange is classically prepared with a long-simmered brown sauce infused with orange and sugar. Here the process is reduced to its simplest form with orange marmalade and soy sauce.

4 SERVINGS

- ⅓ cup orange marmalade
- 2 tablespoons soy sauce
- 1 (4-pound) chicken, rinsed and dried, with giblets removed

1 Preheat the oven to 450°F. In a small bowl, mix the marmalade with the soy sauce. Set the orange glaze aside.

2 Season the cavity of the chicken liberally with salt and pepper. Carefully loosen the skin by running your fingers under the skin of the breast and legs, separating it gently from the meat underneath without tearing it. Spoon half the orange glaze under the skin of the breast and legs.

3 Place the chicken, breast-side down, on a rack set above a rimmed sheet pan or baking dish and roast for 15 minutes. Brush the outside of the chicken with some of the orange glaze and roast for 10 minutes longer.

4 Turn the chicken breast-side up. Roast for another 30 to 35 minutes, until the juices from the thigh run clear, basting with more of the orange glaze every 7 minutes, until it has all been used. Allow to rest for 5 minutes before carving.

Finger-Lickin' Oven-Fried Chicken

The three ingredients in this easy recipe make magic together. The stuffing has all the seasoning needed for a perfect savory crust. The vinegar in the salad dressing adds tang, and the oil coats the chicken, adheres the crumbs, and crisps them as the chicken bakes, helping the chicken to "fry" in the oven with a minimum of fat and a maximum of flavor.

4 SERVINGS

4 pounds chicken parts, skinned

1 cup creamy garlic salad dressing

1½ cups (3½ ounces) seasoned stuffing mix

1   In a mixing bowl, toss the chicken with the dressing. Cover and refrigerate from 1 to 24 hours.

2   Preheat the oven to 450°F. Pulverize the stuffing with a rolling pin or in a blender or food processor until finely ground. Transfer to a large plate, pie plate, or a sheet of wax paper.

3   Lift the chicken from its marinade and roll each piece in the stuffing until well coated. You may have to do this several times to get a thorough coating.

4   Arrange the chicken pieces in a single layer in a nonstick, glass, or ceramic baking pan. Bake for 45 to 50 minutes, until brown and crisp.

Baked Hot Lips Jalapeño Chicken

Hot peppers and corn bread are meant for each other. Here the peppers are part of a commercially prepared dip that's slathered over the chicken, and the corn bread is in the crumbs. Together they form a crust that crisps as it bakes, protecting the chicken and allowing you to cook it without any fatty skin.

4 SERVINGS

- **4 pounds chicken parts, skinned**
- **4 to 5 tablespoons jalapeño ranch dip**
- **1½ cups (3½ ounces) corn bread stuffing mix**

1 In a mixing bowl, toss the chicken with the dip. Cover and refrigerate from 1 to 24 hours.

2 Preheat the oven to 450°F. Pulverize the stuffing with a rolling pin or in a blender or food processor until finely ground. Transfer to a large plate, pie plate, or a sheet of wax paper.

3 Lift the chicken from its marinade and roll each piece in the stuffing until well coated. You may have to do this several times to get a thorough coating.

4 Arrange the chicken pieces in a single layer in a nonstick, glass, or ceramic baking pan. Bake for 45 to 50 minutes until brown and crisp.

Crispy Pecan-Crusted Chicken

The pecans toast as the chicken bakes, transforming the nuts into an exceptionally rich and crunchy crust.

4 SERVINGS

- **4 pounds chicken parts, skinned**
- **1 cup creamy garlic dressing**
- **2 cups (about 5½ ounces) finely ground pecans**

1   In a mixing bowl, toss the chicken with the dressing. Cover and refrigerate from 1 to 24 hours.

2   Preheat the oven to 450°F. Lift the chicken from its marinade and roll each piece in the ground pecans until well coated.

3   Arrange the chicken pieces in a single layer in a nonstick, glass, or ceramic baking dish. Bake for 40 to 45 minutes, until brown and crisp.

Baked Chicken with Molasses-Mustard Glaze

The dark-roasted sugar nuance of molasses is the perfect foil for the spice of brown mustard. Here the two make a pungent glaze for chicken. I bake the chicken first to dry its skin and release some of its fat; both help the glaze to coat the skin more completely.

4 SERVINGS

- **4 pounds chicken parts, rinsed and dried**
- **⅔ cup molasses**
- **⅓ cup spicy brown mustard**

1   Preheat the oven to 450°F. Season the chicken with salt and pepper and arrange it in a single layer in a nonstick, glass, or ceramic baking dish. Bake for 20 minutes, or until the skin loses it raw look.

2   Meanwhile, mix the molasses with the mustard. Spoon off any excess fat in the pan. Pour about two-thirds of the molasses mixture over the chicken and turn to coat.

3   Bake for 25 minutes for breasts or 35 minutes for thighs, basting with some of the sauce in the pan every 5 to 7 minutes. Place the chicken on a serving plate and spoon a portion of the remaining sauce on each piece.

Smoky Hot Pepper Chicken

Chipotle chiles are smoked jalapeño peppers. They are wickedly hot and thick with smoke. Chipotles are available dried, canned packed in tomato adobo sauce, or pureed into hot sauce. This recipe calls for the canned variety. You will only need one to permeate this chicken with both the heat and aroma of a roaring fire.

4 SERVINGS

- **4 pounds chicken parts, rinsed and dried**
- **1 chipotle chile in adobo sauce**
- **2 cups pasta sauce with sweet peppers**

1   Preheat the oven to 450°F. Season the chicken with salt and pepper and arrange in a single layer in a nonstick, glass, or ceramic baking dish. Bake for 20 minutes, or until the skin loses its raw look.

2   Meanwhile, in a blender or food processor combine the chipotle with 1 tablespoon of the adobo sauce in which it was packed and the pasta sauce. Puree until smooth.

3   Spoon off any fat from the pan. Pour the chipotle sauce over the chicken and turn to coat. Bake for 25 minutes for breasts or 35 minutes for thighs, basting with some of the sauce in the pan every 5 to 7 minutes. Place the chicken on a serving plate and spoon a portion of sauce over each piece.

Chicken Slathered in Roasted Garlic

When roasted, garlic turns caramel sweet without losing its garlicky punch. It also melts into an elixir that's perfect for smearing on bread or slathering over baked chicken. The flavor of the garlic is so intriguing that it needs nothing but a little oil to create a complex, redolent glaze.

4 SERVINGS

- **2 large heads of garlic**
- **5 tablespoons extra-virgin olive oil**
- **4 pounds chicken parts, rinsed and dried**

1 Peel the extra papery layers from the outside of the heads of garlic, but do not expose any of the cloves. Rub the heads of garlic with 1 tablespoon of the oil and place in a 2-cup glass measure with ½ cup water. Cover tightly with microwave-safe plastic wrap and microwave on high power for 7 to 8 minutes. The garlic can also be roasted with the oil and water in a pie plate at 400°F for 30 minutes. Cut the heads of garlic in half across their widest perimeter. Squeeze the garlic from the skins into a small bowl. Mash with a fork and mix in the remaining olive oil. Season to taste with salt and pepper.

2 Preheat the oven to 450°F. Rub half the garlic paste under the skin of the chicken pieces. Rub the rest over the skin. Arrange in a single layer in a nonstick, glass, or ceramic baking dish.

3 Bake the chicken for 40 to 45 minutes for breasts or 50 to 55 minutes for thighs, basting with some of the drippings in the pan every 10 minutes.

Mahogany Chicken Wings

The dark red hue of soy creates intense color here, and molasses adds to the roasted sweet flavor of these winning wings. Easy to prepare, they can be munched on at room temperature for an appetizer, or downed by the pile for a casual wing fest.

4 SERVINGS

- **3 pounds chicken wings, rinsed and dried**
- **6 tablespoons teriyaki sauce**
- **¼ cup molasses**

1   Trim the wings of their tip joints (discard these or save for making chicken soup) and separate the remaining sections at the joint.

2   In a large skillet, mix the teriyaki sauce with the molasses and ¼ cup water. Add the chicken wings and toss to coat. Bring to a simmer over medium-high heat. Reduce the heat to medium, cover, and cook for 5 minutes.

3   Uncover and continue cooking, tossing the wings periodically to help them color evenly, until they are no longer pink in the center and the liquid in the pan reduces enough to coat them, 10 to 15 minutes. It may be necessary to lower the heat as the liquid thickens to keep it from scorching. Serve the wings warm or at room temperature.

Broiled Hot Pepper Honey Hens

A game hen is nothing more than a miniature chicken, small enough to broil without fearing that the meat may not cook through. The sauce is made from two ingredients that blend together so seamlessly you will never be able to separate them on the palate. The effect is at once sharp, tangy, sweet, and hot. Don't expose the sauce directly to the flame, or it will lose its flavor.

4 SERVINGS

2 game hens, rinsed and split

½ cup honey

3 tablespoons mild hot pepper sauce, such as Durkee Red Hot

1   Season the underside of the hen halves with salt and pepper. Place skin-side down on a broiler pan and broil 4 inches from a hot fire for 10 to 12 minutes, until deeply browned.

2   Meanwhile, mix the honey and hot sauce together. Brush the cooked side of the game hen halves with some of this mixture and turn over.

3   Broil the hens skin-side up for 8 to 10 minutes, until well browned and cooked through. Remove from the heat. Immediately brush with a heavy coat of the hot pepper honey and set aside to rest for 5 minutes.

Grilled Chicken Breasts with Roasted Pepper Relish

The combination of garlic, roasted peppers, and briny olives lends all the complexity of Mediterranean cooking to this easy relish. Scoop it onto grilled chicken, roast chicken, or other meats and fish.

4 SERVINGS

- **1 jar (6 ounces) roasted red peppers, drained**
- **20 garlic-stuffed green olives plus some of the brine**
- **4 skinless, boneless chicken breast halves, trimmed**

1   Finely chop the roasted peppers and olives in a food processor or with a large knife. Mix in 2 tablespoons of the olive brine and season to taste with salt and pepper. Set the relish aside.

2   Place the chicken breasts between sheets of plastic wrap and pound to a uniform thickness of about ½ inch. Season on both sides with salt and pepper to taste.

3   Grill over a hot fire or broil 4 inches from the heat until browned and firm, about 2 to 3 minutes per side. Serve the grilled breast halves topped with a few spoonfuls of the relish.

Grilled Chicken Breasts with Artichoke Salsa

Two of the great contemporary convenience foods, marinated artichoke hearts and flavored diced tomatoes, come together to form this sprightly salsa. The combination is so good and is so effortless that you'll wonder why you try to "cook" anymore.

4 SERVINGS

- **1 jar (6 ounces) marinated artichoke hearts, marinade reserved**
- **3 tablespoons canned diced tomatoes with jalapeños (salsa style)**
- **4 skinless, boneless chicken breast halves, trimmed**

1   Finely chop the artichoke hearts in a food processor or with a large knife. Add the tomatoes and chop until the tomatoes are coarsely chopped. Mix in 1 tablespoon of the reserved artichoke marinade. Season to taste with salt and pepper. Set the salsa aside.

2   Place the chicken breasts between sheets of plastic wrap and pound to a uniform thickness of about ½ inch. Brush lightly with some of the remaining artichoke marinade.

3   Grill over a hot fire or broil 4 inches from the heat until browned and firm, about 2 to 3 minutes per side. Serve the grilled breast halves, each topped with a few spoonfuls of the salsa.

Meaty Matters

Buffalo Burgers

Mexican Meat Loaf

Creamy Turkey Meat Loaf

Cider-Braised Turkey Breast

Steak au Poivre

Sirloin Steak with Balsamic
  Glaze

Beef Paprikash

Beef Stewed with Wild
  Mushrooms

Veal Chops Piccata

Calf's Liver in Raspberry Glaze

Pork Chops Piquant

Roast Pork in Mustard Crumbs

Chinese Barbecued Ribs

Leg of Lamb Niçoise

Garlic-Braised Lamb

Buffalo Burgers

These are great! The butter and hot sauce blend with the meat juices to make a truly extraordinary burger. If you feel the need to gild this lily, a crumbling of blue cheese will turn it into the most unusual and tastiest cheeseburger you've ever had.

4 SERVINGS

- **1 pound ground beef**
- **2 tablespoons butter**
- **2 tablespoons mild hot pepper sauce, such as Durkee Red Hot**

1   Mix the ground beef with 3 tablespoons cold water, ¼ teaspoon salt, and ⅛ teaspoon pepper. Form into 4 burgers about ½ inch thick.

2   Grill over a hot fire or broil 4 inches from the heat to desired doneness, 8 to 15 minutes, depending upon heat source and taste preferences.

3   Meanwhile, in a small saucepan, melt the butter over medium-low heat. Remove from the heat and mix in the hot sauce. Brush the sauce all over the cooked burgers.

Mexican Meat Loaf

There are two tricks to this meat loaf. One is the use of meat loaf mix—a blend of ground beef, veal, and pork—that you can buy in any butcher shop or supermarket. The beef adds flavor, the veal lends moisture, and the pork contributes richness. The other trick is the large amount of bread crumbs and liquid in the ingredients. What makes some meat loaves dry and heavy is that they have too much meat and not enough filler. Meat may be the main attraction, but it is everything else that gives the loaf flavor, texture, and lightness.

6 SERVINGS

1 cup thick salsa (medium or hot)

1 cup seasoned bread crumbs

2 pounds ground meat loaf mixture

1 Preheat the oven to 375°F. Chop the salsa finely in a food processor or blender. In a mixing bowl, blend the salsa with the bread crumbs and ½ cup cold water. Set aside for 10 minutes.

2 Add the meat to the salsa mixture and combine thoroughly with your hands. Season with ¼ teaspoon salt and ⅛ teaspoon pepper. Form into a rough loaf on a rimmed sheet pan, in a 6-cup casserole, or in a 9-by-5-inch loaf pan.

3 Bake the meat loaf for 1 hour.

Creamy Turkey Meat Loaf

 Ground turkey is very low in fat, a quality that may make your nutritionist swoon, but can send your taste buds packing. This deficiency is replaced by the oil in the dressing. It's less saturated than meat fat, which makes it healthier, while providing the same sensory qualities. Unlike many turkey meat loaves, which do back flips in an attempt to imitate beef, this recipe basks in the mild creamy texture and flavor that a red-meat meat loaf could never attain.

6 SERVINGS

1 cup corn bread stuffing mix

1 cup ranch dressing

2 pounds ground turkey

1 Preheat the oven to 375°F. Pulverize the stuffing mix with a rolling pin or in a blender or food processor. In a large bowl, mix the stuffing crumbs with the ranch dressing and ½ cup cold water. Set aside for 10 minutes.

2 Add the ground turkey to the stuffing mixture and combine thoroughly with your hands. Season with ¼ teaspoon salt and ⅛ teaspoon pepper. Form into a rough loaf on a rimmed sheet pan, in a 6-cup casserole, or in a 9-by-5-inch loaf pan.

3 Bake the turkey meat loaf for 1 hour.

Cider-Braised Turkey Breast

This turkey breast is cooked in record time by simmering it in apple cider rather than roasting it the traditional way. As it bubbles, the tang of the cider intensifies, blending with the juices of the turkey into a sweet and savory sauce. Serve with a stovetop bread stuffing or buttered broad egg noodles.

4 SERVINGS

- **2 pounds skinless, boneless turkey breast**
- **2 tablespoons minced garlic in oil**
- **3 cups apple cider**

1 Rub the turkey breast with salt and pepper and half the garlic in oil, using as much of the oil as possible. Place a large nonstick skillet over medium-high heat for 1 minute. Add the turkey and cook in the hot dry skillet, turning, until browned on both sides, about 1 minute per side.

2 Reduce the heat to low. Add the remaining minced garlic and the cider. Stir, scraping up any brown bits clinging to the bottom of the pan. Cover and simmer gently for 45 minutes, turning the turkey every 10 minutes, until the thickest part of the meat registers 165°F on an instant-read thermometer.

3 Uncover the pan. Remove the turkey to a cutting board and allow to rest for 10 minutes. Meanwhile, boil the juices in the pan over high heat until reduced to 1 cup. Slice the turkey crosswise on a diagonal and serve with the sauce.

Steak au Poivre

My rendition of pepper steak is covered with multicolored mixed peppercorns. This highly aromatic pepper is sold in gourmet stores, spice shops, and most supermarkets. The peppercorns are only available whole, but can be cracked in a mortar and pestle or in a peppermill set on its coarsest setting. Once cracked, the peppercorns are pressed into only one side of the steak, to keep them from overpowering the meat.

4 SERVINGS

- **2 pounds sirloin, porterhouse, or rib eye steak(s), cut 1 inch thick**
- **1½ tablespoons cracked mixed peppercorns**
- **3 tablespoons unsalted butter**

1 Season the steak(s) with salt. Press the cracked pepper into one side of the steak(s).

2 Melt 1 tablespoon of the butter in a large nonstick skillet over medium-high heat. When sizzling, add the steak(s), pepper-side down, and cook 4 to 5 minutes per side for rare, 6 to 7 minutes per side for medium, and 8 or more minutes per side for well done.

3 Transfer the meat to a platter. Remove the pan from the heat and let cool for 1 minute. Swirl in the remaining butter and pour over the steak(s).

Sirloin Steak with Balsamic Glaze

Balsamic vinegar, the aged, sweet mahogany-colored wine vinegar from Modena, is at its best paired with meats. Here it deglazes the surface of a grilled steak, intensifying its beefy flavors and counterpointing its rich marbling.

4 SERVINGS

- **2 pounds sirloin steak, cut 1 inch thick**
- **1 tablespoon minced garlic in oil**
- **2 tablespoons balsamic vinegar**

1   Rub the steak with salt, pepper, and the garlic. Grill over a hot fire or broil 4 inches from the heat, 4 to 5 minutes per side for rare, 6 to 8 minutes per side for medium, and 9 to 11 minutes per side for well-done.

2   Remove to a platter and let rest for 3 minutes. Mix the juices that collect on the plate with the vinegar and spoon over the steak.

Beef Paprikash

This is a remarkable recipe: a pot full of onions is simmered slowly, turning the liquid into a sweet, pungent broth. After a while, stewing beef joins the onion elixir, absorbing its caramelized aroma along with a hefty dose of ground sweet red pepper (paprika). The finished concoction is more confection than stew. If desired, serve over noodles or with dumplings.

4 SERVINGS

- **4 large Vidalia, Maui, or Bermuda onions, halved and thinly sliced**
- **2 pounds marinated London broil (see Note)**
- **3 tablespoons Hungarian paprika**

1 Place the onions in a large heavy pot with ½ cup water. Cook, stirring often, until they become very soft, about 10 minutes.

2 Meanwhile, prepare a hot fire in a grill or preheat a broiler. Scrape off as much marinade as possible from the meat and reserve. Grill or broil the meat until browned on both sides, about 4 minutes per side. Cut into 1-inch cubes.

3 Add the meat, reserved marinade, paprika, and salt and pepper to taste to the onions. Cover and cook over low heat for 2½ hours, until the onions have cooked down into a sauce and the meat is very tender. Season with additional salt and pepper to taste before serving.

NOTE Most butchers and many supermarkets sell London broils marinated in barbecue sauce alongside the fresh London broils.

Beef Stewed with Wild Mushrooms

Wild mushrooms contribute a wonderful dark, rich taste to this stew. I've called for dried mushrooms here, which can be bought year-round and stored indefinitely in a cupboard. Serve over brown rice pilaf or kasha, if desired.

4 SERVINGS

1 ounce dried wild mushrooms—shiitakes, porcini, or dried imported mushrooms

2 pounds boneless stewing beef, such as chuck or bottom round, cut into 1½-inch chunks

2 cups vegetable cocktail juice

1 In a medium mixing bowl, soak the dried mushrooms in 2 cups hot water for 20 minutes, until soft and plump. Remove the mushrooms from the liquid, gently squeezing any extra water back into the bowl. Rinse briefly to remove any grit. If using shiitakes, cut off the stems. Coarsely chop the mushrooms. Strain the soaking liquid through a coffee filter or fine sieve and reserve separately.

2 Season the beef with salt and pepper. Cook on a hot grill pan or under a preheated broiler, turning, until browned, 6 to 8 minutes.

3 Transfer the meat to a large heavy saucepan or flameproof casserole. Add the mushroom soaking liquid and vegetable juice. Bring to a boil, reduce the heat to medium-low, cover, and simmer for 45 minutes.

4 Add the chopped mushrooms. Season the stew to taste with salt and pepper and simmer 30 minutes longer, or until the beef is very tender and the sauce is slightly thickened.

Veal Chops Piccata

This recipe borrows its piquant fruity sauce from veal piccata and utilizes it as a glaze for grilled veal chops. I would serve these with a side of spinach and spaghetti.

4 SERVINGS

- **1 lemon**
- **2 teaspoons minced garlic in oil**
- **4 veal rib chops (8 ounces each)**

1 Remove the zest from the lemon with a zester or grater. If removed with a zester, chop finely. Mix the zest with the garlic and ¼ teaspoon each salt and pepper. Rub into both sides of the veal chops. Let rest for 10 minutes.

2 Grill or broil 4 inches from a medium flame to the desired degree of doneness, about 4 minutes per side for rare, 5 minutes per side for medium, and 6 to 7 minutes per side for well-done.

3 Place on a platter, season with more salt and pepper, and squeeze the lemon over top.

Calf's Liver in Raspberry Glaze

If you think liver tastes bitter and grainy, you have never had it cooked properly. The trick is to slice it very thinly and cook it over high heat as quickly as possible. As soon as it is browned, it is done. This recipe matches the richness of calf's liver with a sweet fruit vinegar.

4 SERVINGS

- **1 pound calf's liver, trimmed and thinly sliced**
- **3 tablespoons unsalted butter**
- **⅓ cup raspberry vinegar**

1   Season the liver with salt and pepper.

2   Melt half the butter in a large nonstick skillet over high heat. Add the liver and cook just until browned outside but still rosy inside, about 1 to 1½ minutes per side. Remove from the heat and arrange the liver on plates.

3   Add the remaining butter to the pan and swirl to melt. Add the vinegar, swirl to combine, and pour over the liver. Serve at once.

Pork Chops Piquant

These chops veritably glow with their sauce that is part jalapeño and part tangy vinaigrette. There are many varieties of sun-dried tomato dressings. Any one will do, but the hot pepper sauce must be the green Tabasco, made from mild jalapeño peppers. The flavor of this sauce is remarkable, sweet, fiery, and brimming with the aroma of fresh green vegetables.

4 SERVINGS

- **4 pork chops, cut ¾ inch thick**
- **1 cup sun-dried tomato salad dressing**
- **4 teaspoons Jalapeño Tabasco sauce**

1 Season the chops on both sides with salt and pepper. Heat a large nonstick skillet over high heat for 1 minute. Brown the chops in the hot skillet, about 2 minutes per side.

2 Add ½ cup water to the pan. Reduce the heat to medium, cover, and steam until water is mostly evaporated, about 4 minutes.

3 Add the dressing and jalapeño Tabasco sauce and heat to a simmer. Remove from the heat, cover, and set aside for 5 minutes. Serve the chops topped with the sauce.

Roast Pork in Mustard Crumbs

Mustard is a favorite condiment with meat. Here it is slathered over a pork roast to hold a crisp crust of uniquely seasoned bread crumbs to its surface. The crumbs are pulverized salad croutons, which have a buttery richness that other bread crumbs lack.

4 SERVINGS

- **2 pounds boneless pork loin, rolled and tied**
- **1 cup garlic croutons, ground**
- **2 tablespoons spicy brown mustard**

1 Preheat the oven to 400°F. Season the pork generously all over with salt and pepper. Place on a rack set in a roasting pan and roast for 30 minutes. Remove from the oven and set aside for 10 minutes to cool. Reduce the oven temperature to 350°F.

2 Meanwhile, grind the croutons finely in a food processor or blender, and place in a pie pan. Brush the pork all over with a thick layer of mustard and roll it in the crumbs to coat.

3 Return the pork to the rack in the pan and roast 30 minutes longer, or until the internal temperature of the meat registers 160°F to 165°F. Let stand for 10 minutes before slicing.

Chinese Barbecued Ribs

Baby back ribs grill in half the time of full-size ribs, and they need no precooking to tenderize them. These take on a rich dark lacquer from a glaze of duck sauce mixed with teriyaki sauce.

4 SERVINGS

- **2 pounds baby back ribs**
- **½ cup sweet and sour duck sauce**
- **¼ cup teriyaki sauce**

1 Season the ribs generously with salt and pepper on all sides. Grill over a medium fire until lightly browned, about 4 minutes per side.

2 Meanwhile, mix the duck sauce and teriyaki sauce together. Brush the glaze over the ribs and turn them. Continue turning the ribs and brushing them with glaze every 3 minutes, until the ribs are evenly browned and tender, about 15 to 20 minutes.

3 Cut the ribs into individual pieces. Serve hot.

Leg of Lamb Niçoise

Leg of lamb is one of the most succulent of roasts, and this recipe takes it to its flavorful apex. First garlic, which is essential and ubiquitous with lamb, is rubbed into the meat; but it is the anchovies that are a real surprise. Their salty pungency melds with the full flavor of the lamb in ways that make the two ingredients forever altered and inseparable. I would serve this lamb with roasted potatoes and buttered green beans.

8 SERVINGS

- **1 tin (2 ounces) flat anchovy fillets in oil**
- **1 tablespoon minced garlic in oil**
- **5- to 6-pound boneless leg of lamb, rolled and tied**

1   Mince the anchovies and reserve the oil in which they are packed. Mix the anchovies with the garlic and season with salt and pepper. Season the lamb all over with salt and pepper. Rub with the garlic and anchovy mixture. Wrap in plastic and refrigerate for several hours or overnight.

2   Preheat the oven to 450°F. Place the lamb on a rack in a roasting pan and roast for 30 minutes. Reduce the heat to 375°F and continue to roast for 1 to 1½ hours longer. Test for doneness. When medium rare, the lamb will register between 135°F and 140°F. Medium will be 145°F to 150°F. Remove the lamb from the oven and let stand for 10 minutes before slicing. Drizzle with the reserved anchovy oil before serving.

Garlic-Braised Lamb

If you like lamb chops, but not the price, shoulder chops are the cut for you. They cost a fraction of what loin and rib chops sell for, simply because they aren't as tender. But what they lack in tenderness, they make up for in flavor.

Here the chops are browned on a grill or in a broiler, and then simmered to tenderness with lots of garlic and vegetable cocktail juice that blends with the meaty flavor of the chops into a full-flavored gravy. Serve with garlic mashed potatoes, noodles, or rice pilaf.

4 TO 6 SERVINGS

3 pounds lamb shoulder chops or lamb stew meat

2 tablespoons minced garlic in oil

2 cups vegetable cocktail juice

1   Season the lamb lightly with salt and pepper and rub with 1 tablespoon of the minced garlic in oil. Broil or grill until browned on both sides, 2 to 3 minutes per side.

2   In a nonreactive Dutch oven, mix the vegetable juice with 1 cup of water and the remaining garlic. Bring to a simmer over low heat.

3   Add the browned meat and ¼ teaspoon each salt and pepper. Simmer until the meat is tender, about 45 minutes. Skim the fat from the liquid before serving.

Simply Seafood

Bluefish with Creamy Horseradish Sauce

Blackened Fish Fillets

Fresh Tuna Braised with Caramelized Onions

Lemon Poppyseed Salmon

Grilled Fish with Feta Vinaigrette

Tea-Smoked Fish

Caesar-Baked Fish

Ginger Sake Fish Steak

Seared Scallops in Caper Brown Butter

Baked Sesame Scallops

Spiced Grilled Shrimp

Instant Scampi

Grilled Soft-Shell Crabs with Fresh Orange Sauce

Ginger Black Bean Clams

Creole Oysters

Bluefish with Creamy Horseradish Sauce

Horseradish is harsh and can easily overwhelm any other ingredient it touches, but not bluefish. The pair are a perfect match, each balancing the intense flavor of the other. Because horseradish loses flavor with heat, it is added to the fish juices after the bluefish is done baking.

4 SERVINGS

- ½ cup ranch dressing
- ¼ cup prepared white horseradish
- 1½ pounds bluefish fillet, skinned

1 Remove the dressing and horseradish from the refrigerator. Preheat the oven to 375°F. Season the fish lightly on both sides with salt and pepper. Place in a baking dish large enough to hold the fillets in a single layer.

2 Bake for 12 to 15 minutes, until the thickest part of the bluefish flakes to gentle pressure. With a wide spatula, transfer the fish to a serving platter.

3 Add the ranch dressing and horseradish to the drippings in the baking dish. Stir to incorporate and pour over the fish.

Blackened Fish Fillets

The most important ingredient in blackening isn't an ingredient at all. It's heat: intense and unbridled, and strong enough to spin spices into culinary gold. You will need to use a large (at least 12-inch) iron skillet, and heat it until its surface turns ashen, about 8 minutes over high heat. If the fish flames for a second when it hits the pan, don't worry. It's only the oil on the surface of the fish, and it will die down in seconds.

4 SERVINGS

- **4 (6-ounce) fish fillets, such as catfish, orange roughy, St. Peter's fish, red fish, sea bass**
- **3 tablespoons vegetable oil**
- **2 tablespoons plus 2 teaspoons Cajun spice blend, such as Paul Prudhomme's Fish Magic**

1 Brush the fish with half the oil. Sprinkle 1 teaspoon of Cajun spices over each side of the fillets. Refrigerate for 1 hour.

2 Heat a large cast-iron skillet over high heat (or over an outside grill) for 7 to 8 minutes. Turn the hood exhaust fan on high.

3 Coat the fish with the remaining oil. Add to the preheated pan and cook for 1 to 2 minutes per side, depending on the thickness of the fillets. *Warning: the fish may flash-flame when it hits the pan, and it will smoke vigorously as it cooks.*

Fresh Tuna Braised with Caramelized Onions

This simple dish is remarkably tasty. The sugar in the onions caramelizes, creating a multitude of savory and sweet flavors that play off the meatiness of the tuna. Sauté the tuna just long enough to brown its surfaces, leaving more time for it to simmer with the onions and develop the desired flavors. If you can't find fresh tuna in your market, swordfish, monkfish, or shark would make a good substitute.

4 SERVINGS

2 tablespoons olive oil

4 (7- or 8-ounce) tuna steaks, dark parts trimmed off

2 large Vidalia or other sweet onions, peeled, quartered, and thinly sliced

1 In a large skillet, heat half the oil over high heat. Season the tuna steaks liberally with salt and pepper and brown on both sides, about 1 minute per side. Remove to a plate.

2 Add the remaining oil to the pan and reduce the heat to medium-low. Add the onions and season with salt and pepper. Cook, stirring occasionally, until golden, about 4 minutes. Cover the pan and cook 6 minutes longer, until the onions are very soft and lightly browned.

3 Return the tuna to the pan and cook for 4 minutes per side. Serve the tuna steaks garnished with the onions.

Lemon Poppyseed Salmon

This exceptionally easy salmon is perfumed with lemon zest, the colored part of the peel. In addition to its tangy sweet and sour flavor, you'll enjoy the dish's texture, which contrasts the silky salmon with the crunch from a crackled crust of poppyseeds.

4 SERVINGS

- **1 lemon**
- **½ cup poppyseed dressing**
- **4 (8-ounce) salmon steaks**

1   Remove the zest from the lemon with a zester or fine-tooth grater. If using a zester, chop the strips of zest finely. Mix the zest with the lemon juice and the poppyseed dressing. Pour half this mixture over the fish steaks. Turn to coat, cover, and refrigerate for 20 minutes.

2   Remove the fish from its marinade. Grill or broil 4 inches from a high flame for 3 to 4 minutes per side, until the fish is barely firm. Pour the remaining poppyseed dressing over the fish and serve.

Grilled Fish with Feta Vinaigrette

Salad dressing is the best kept grilling secret. A simple vinaigrette has all the ingredients necessary to flavor grilled foods and keep them moist. Here half the vinaigrette is used for marinating and basting, while the remainder seasons a fresh feta cheese sauce.

4 SERVINGS

4 (8-ounce) firm-fleshed fish steaks, such as salmon, swordfish, or tuna

½ cup Italian dressing

4 ounces feta cheese, crumbled

1 Rub the fish steaks with half the dressing, cover, and refrigerate for 1 hour.

2 Mix the remaining dressing with the feta cheese. Set the feta vinaigrette aside.

3 Remove the fish from the marinade and grill or broil 4 inches from a high flame for 3 to 4 minutes per side, until the fish is barely firm. Pour the feta vinaigrette over the fish and serve.

Tea-Smoked Fish

Tea seasons this fish on two fronts. First, it is a marinade that permeates the seafood with the familiar flavor of brewed tea. Then, during cooking, the same acrid flavors turn aromatic, as the tea leaves provide a cloud of smoke that envelops the grilling fish.

4 SERVINGS

- **¼ cup loose black tea leaves, such as English Breakfast or Earl Grey**
- **¼ cup ginger preserves**
- **4 (8-ounce) firm-fleshed fish steaks, such as salmon, swordfish, or tuna**

1 Steep the tea in ½ cup boiling water for 1 minute. Add ½ cup cold water and steep 1 minute longer. Strain the liquid from the tea leaves into a flat high-sided dish. Reserve the tea leaves. Mix half the preserves with the liquid tea and season with salt and pepper. Cover and marinate the fish steaks for 1 hour.

2 Light a hot fire in a covered barbecue grill. Mix the reserved tea leaves with the remaining ginger preserves on a large sheet of heavy-duty aluminum foil. Set directly on the coals of the barbecue grill and allow to preheat until the tea is smoking, about 3 minutes.

3 Remove the fish from the marinade and cook on a rack set 4 inches above the smoking tea leaves. Cover the grill and cook for 3 to 4 minutes per side, until the fish is firm.

Caesar-Baked Fish

The anchovy-garlic-mustard magic of Caesar dressing gilds this fish twice. It infuses the flesh with a Caesar dressing marinade, and it coats the fillets with a crust of crushed Caesar-flavored croutons. Use any firm fish fillet that's suitable for baking, such as salmon, bluefish, swordfish, orange roughy, catfish, or monkfish.

4 SERVINGS

2 cups Caesar-flavored croutons

1½ pounds firm-fleshed fish fillet, about ¾ inch thick

¼ cup plus 2 tablespoons Caesar salad dressing

1 Preheat the oven to 450°F. Pulverize the croutons in a food processor or with a rolling pin. Place on a plate or a sheet of wax paper.

2 Cut the fish into equal serving pieces. Season lightly with salt and pepper. Brush the fish with the dressing and roll in the crouton crumbs until well coated. Set fillets well spaced on a rack on a rimmed sheet pan.

3 Slide into the oven and bake for 10 minutes, until the fish flakes to gentle pressure.

Ginger Sake Fish Steak

There are several ginger-flavored salad dressings on the market. Some are fruity, others have a tomato base, and some are simple vinaigrettes. This recipe is equally delicious with any one.

4 SERVINGS

- **½ cup ginger salad dressing**
- **⅓ cup sake (Japanese rice wine)**
- **4 firm-fleshed fish steaks, such as salmon, tuna, or swordfish, about 1 inch thick**

1 Mix the dressing and sake together. Brush 2 tablespoons of the marinade over each fish steak. Refrigerate for 30 minutes.

2 Broil the fish 2 inches from a hot broiler for 4 to 5 minutes per side, until the fish is browned outside and just opaque in the center.

3 Meanwhile, heat the remaining sauce in a small saucepan. Spoon over the broiled fish and serve.

Seared Scallops in Caper Brown Butter

The biggest mistake people make with scallops is overcooking them. Scallops come from the toughest muscle in a mollusk. Heat them too long, and they have all the textural appeal of a hockey puck. Here they are cooked quickly, just until they're well browned on both sides. Finished in a flash with butter and capers, this dish is perfect with rice and steamed asparagus. Garnish with lemon wedges if you have a fresh lemon on hand.

4 SERVINGS

- **1 pound large sea scallops, trimmed (see Note)**
- **3 tablespoons butter**
- **2 tablespoons capers**

1 Season the scallops lightly with pepper. Heat 1 tablespoon of the butter in a large nonstick skillet over medium-high heat until foamy. Add the scallops to the hot butter and cook, turning, until lightly browned, about 2 minutes per side.

2 Add the capers and cook 30 seconds. Swirl in the remaining 2 tablespoons butter and remove from the heat. Season the sauce with salt and pepper to taste. Serve the scallops sauced with the caper butter.

NOTE Scallops have already been cleaned when you purchase them, but they may have a sliver of tough tendon attached to one side. This should be removed before cooking. You can peel it off with your fingers.

Baked Sesame Scallops

This ten-minute meal creates a crispy coating on barely baked scallops by heating the oven to its most incendiary heights and cooking the scallops with a shell of toasted sesame seeds.

4 SERVINGS

1½ pounds sea scallops

¼ cup plus 2 tablespoons ranch dressing

1 cup toasted sesame seeds

1   Preheat oven to 450°F. Brush the scallops with the dressing and roll in the sesame seeds until lightly coated.

2   Set well spaced on a rack on a rimmed sheet pan. Slide into the oven and bake for 6 to 8 minutes, until the scallops are barely firm.

Spiced Grilled Shrimp

Old Bay, the classic sweet, salty, savory spice blend that's traditionally used for boiling crabs, seasons a coating of yogurt with unpretentious panache. You will be amazed that three ingredients can supply so much flavor.

4 SERVINGS

- **1½ pounds jumbo (16 to 20 count) shrimp**
- **½ cup plain yogurt**
- **1 tablespoon Old Bay seasoning**

1 With scissors, slit the shrimp shells down the center ridge of the back. Clean the vein from under the slit, but do not remove the shell.

2 Mix the yogurt with the Old Bay. Add the shrimp and toss to coat. Cover and refrigerate for 1 hour.

3 Prepare a hot fire in a barbecue grill. Lightly grease the rack of the grill. Grill the shrimp 4 inches from the heat for 1½ minutes per side, or until pink and curled. Serve hot or at room temperature. Peel or allow everyone to peel their own.

Instant Scampi

Scampi are large saltwater crayfish that populate the Ligurian Sea off the western coast of Italy. We do not get scampi here, but we identify any shrimp dish with an Italian flavor as scampi-style. Here the Italian influence comes from a slew of minced garlic.

4 SERVINGS

- **1½ pounds jumbo (16 to 20 count) shrimp, shelled and deveined**
- **1 tablespoon minced garlic in oil**
- **1 cup dry white wine**

1   In a large nonstick skillet, toss the shrimp with the garlic in oil, ¼ teaspoon salt, and ⅛ teaspoon pepper. Cook over medium-low heat, stirring occasionally, until the shrimp start to sizzle, about 1 minute. They will still look raw.

2   Add the wine, raise the heat to high, and bring to a boil. Remove the shrimp to a serving plate and boil the wine until it is reduced to ¼ cup and is slightly thickened. Adjust the seasoning with more salt and pepper, pour the sauce over the shrimp, and serve.

Grilled Soft-Shell Crabs with Fresh Orange Sauce

Soft-shell crabs are hard-shell blue crabs that have recently molted, leaving behind a slightly leathery skin and succulent meat. The whole crab is edible. Just sauté and serve with a knife and fork. Ask your fish seller to clean them for you.

4 SERVINGS

- **2 oranges**
- **⅓ cup extra-virgin olive oil**
- **8 live soft-shell crabs, cleaned**

1   Remove the zest from the oranges with a zester or the finest teeth of a grater. In a glass or ceramic dish large enough to hold all the crabs in a single layer, mix the orange zest with the olive oil. Squeeze the juice from the oranges into a small bowl and set aside.

2   Wash the crabs well and dry with paper towels. Season on both sides with salt and pepper. Place in the orange-oil mixture and turn to coat. Cover and marinate in the refrigerator for 30 minutes.

3   Light a hot fire in a grill or preheat the broiler. Lift the crabs from the marinade; reserve the marinade. Grill or broil the crabs upside down 4 inches from the heat for 3 to 4 minutes. Baste with marinade. Turn, baste again, and grill 3 to 4 minutes longer, until lightly browned.

4   Meanwhile, mix the reserved orange juice with the remaining marinade in a small saucepan. Bring to a boil. Remove the crabs to a platter, spoon the orange sauce over top, and serve at once.

Ginger Black Bean Clams

Chinese black bean sauce is intense enough to make all other seasonings extraneous. Here the flavors of fresh ginger and the juice from the clams are all else that is required. Do not add salt, because both the bean sauce and the clams are quite salty.

4 SERVINGS

48 littleneck clams

1 inch fresh ginger, cut into thin strips

1 tablespoon Chinese black bean sauce with garlic

1   Place the clams in a large bowl, cover with cold water, and swirl in the water to remove surface dirt; drain. Cover the clams with clean cold water.

2   In a large heavy pot, combine the ginger, black bean sauce, ⅛ teaspoon pepper, and ½ cup water. Bring to a boil over high heat.

3   Drain the clams and add them to the pot. Cover and boil until the clam shells open, about 5 minutes. Serve the clams in the sauce. (Discard any that do not open.)

Creole Oysters

This recipe is the epitome of the three-ingredient concept. Each of its trio of elements plays off the others expertly; they need nothing else. Creole Oysters are best served with bread or toasts to catch the sauce.

4 SERVINGS

1 pint shucked fresh oysters, drained

1 cup heavy cream

2 to 3 teaspoons Tabasco sauce

1 In a medium nonstick skillet, heat the oysters over medium-high heat until they plump, about 2 minutes. Remove them with a slotted spoon. Boil the liquid in the skillet until it is reduced by half. Add the cream and boil until the sauce thickens slightly, about 2 minutes. Stir in the Tabasco.

2 Return the oysters to the skillet and warm through, but do not overcook, or they will toughen and shrink. Serve the oysters and spicy cream in soup plates.

Instant Pasta Sauces

Tomato Vinaigrette

White Clam Sauce

Calamari in Red Sauce

Sardine Tapenade

Pepper Feta Provençal Sauce

Herb Cheese and Spinach Sauce

Garlic, Clam, and Bean Sauce

Classic Alfredo Sauce

Carbonara Sauce

Goat Cheese and Arugula Sauce

Gorgonzola and Walnut Sauce

Bagna Romano

Asparagus, Garlic, and Cheese Sauce

Broccoli Rabe and Garlic Sauce

Tomato and Basil Sauce

Roasted Pepper, Artichoke, and Ricotta Salata Sauce

Sun-Dried Tomato Pesto

Tuna, Dill, and Garlic Sauce

Mussels in Red Sauce

Sausage and Mushroom Sauce

Tomato Vinaigrette

Most of the time oil is used for cooking or for texture, but here it is a seasoning. Stewed tomatoes are reduced and enriched with the olive-rich flavor of extra-virgin oil and the sweet pungency of balsamic vinegar. This recipe works equally well as a pasta salad dressing if you double the vinegar.

ABOUT 2¹/₂ CUPS, ENOUGH FOR 4 SERVINGS WHEN TOSSED WITH 1 POUND PASTA

- **2 cans (14½ ounces each) Italian-style stewed tomatoes**
- **¼ cup extra-virgin olive oil**
- **1 tablespoon balsamic vinegar**

1   Puree the stewed tomatoes in a food processor or blender. Transfer to a heavy, nonreactive 2- to 3-quart saucepan. Simmer over medium-high heat, stirring often, until slightly thickened, about 8 minutes.

2   Stir in the olive oil and vinegar. Season to taste with salt and pepper.

White Clam Sauce

Canned clam sauce has become so commonplace, we have lost track of the fact that the real thing has always been one of the simplest and easiest of all pasta sauces. Because this is a very thin sauce with lots of chunks of clams and garlic, it is best tossed with a shaped pasta that can catch and cradle the sauce.

ABOUT 6 CUPS, ENOUGH FOR 4 SERVINGS
WHEN TOSSED WITH 1 POUND PASTA

48 littleneck clams

¼ cup olive oil

2 cloves garlic, minced

1   Place the clams in a large bowl, cover with cold water, and swirl in the water to remove surface dirt; drain. Cover the clams with fresh water. Refrigerate 1 hour.

2   In a large saucepan, heat the olive oil over medium heat. Drain the clams and add to the hot oil. Add the garlic and plenty of pepper. Cover and cook for about 4 minutes, until the clams open. (Discard any that do not open.) Adjust the seasoning with salt, if needed.

Calamari in Red Sauce

If you are squeamish about squid, don't be. Of all seafoods, it is the least fishy and one of the easiest to appreciate. And now that cleaned squid is commonly sold in supermarkets, there is no reason not to include it in your dinner repertoire. The trick is to cook the squid fast and very briefly. After only a few minutes of simmering, a sliced squid will vulcanize into a pile of rubber bands.

ABOUT 2 1/2 CUPS SAUCE, ENOUGH FOR 4 SERVINGS WHEN TOSSED WITH 1 POUND PASTA

- **14 sun-dried tomatoes in oil, finely chopped, 1 tablespoon oil reserved**
- **1 pound cleaned squid, bodies sliced into rings, tentacles cut in half**
- **3 tablespoons chopped fresh basil**

1 In a medium skillet, heat the reserved oil from the tomatoes over high heat. Add the squid and cook, tossing, until it loses its raw look, about 30 seconds.

2 Reduce the heat to medium and add the sun-dried tomatoes and basil. Cook until the squid is firm, 1 to 2 minutes. Season with salt and pepper to taste and serve at once.

Sardine Tapenade

If the notion of olives and sardines sends you running for cover, you're not alone. The day I tested this recipe, everyone in my family turned up their noses at the mere thought of it. Out of obligation they tasted, and before I knew it the bowl was clean. Because it uses canned ingredients, there is no cooking. Just combine everything and let the warmth of the pasta do the rest.

ABOUT $^1/_2$ CUP, ENOUGH FOR 4 SERVINGS
WHEN TOSSED WITH 1 POUND PASTA

- **¼ cup black olive paste**
- **2 cloves garlic, minced**
- **1 tin (3¾ ounces) sardines packed in olive oil, oil reserved.**

Mix together the olive paste, garlic, and sardines with their oil. Season with plenty of pepper. Add ½ cup pasta cooking water when tossing the sauce with pasta.

Pepper Feta Provençal Sauce

This pungent creamy sauce is indelibly rich and incredibly easy. All you do is mix the ingredients together, but the results are bursting with Mediterranean flavor.

ABOUT 1½ CUPS, ENOUGH FOR 4 SERVINGS WHEN TOSSED WITH 1 POUND PASTA

- **1 package (7 ounces) feta cheese with black or hot pepper**
- **10 sun-dried tomatoes in oil, finely chopped**
- **2 teaspoons black olive paste**

1 Mix all the ingredients together. Season with salt and pepper to taste.

2 When the pasta is cooked, reserve ½ cup of the cooking water. Add it when you toss the pasta with the sauce.

Herb Cheese and Spinach Sauce

The only hassle to cooking spinach is getting rid of the water that seeps from the softening leaves. My suggestion is to take advantage of it. In this recipe, it thins an herb-flavored cream cheese to a perfect saucy consistency. To save time, you can use packaged pre-washed and stemmed spinach here, but be sure to dunk it into a bowl of water before adding it to the skillet.

ABOUT 1 CUP, ENOUGH FOR 4 SERVINGS
WHEN TOSSED WITH 1 POUND PASTA

2 tablespoons extra-virgin olive oil

10 ounces fresh spinach, stemmed and washed (not dried)

4 ounces herb and garlic cream cheese

1 Heat the olive oil in a medium skillet over medium-high heat. Add the wet spinach and cover the pan. Cook until the spinach is wilted, 1 to 2 minutes.

2 Add in the cream cheese and stir until melted. Season to taste with salt and pepper.

Garlic, Clam, and Bean Sauce

One of the most incompatible pasta and sauce combinations has to be spaghetti and clam sauce. Not a speck of the sauce has a chance of clinging to the noodle. This recipe corrects the problem by teaming clams with beans, a classic northern Italian combination. The beans thicken the sauce, causing it to coat the pasta without adding a speck of unwanted fat.

ABOUT 1 1/2 CUPS, ENOUGH FOR 4 SERVINGS
WHEN TOSSED WITH 1 POUND PASTA

- **1 bottle (15 ounces) white clam sauce**
- **2 cloves garlic, minced**
- **1 cup cooked or canned navy beans, drained and rinsed**

1   In a small saucepan, combine the clam sauce and garlic. Bring to a boil over medium heat.

2   Stir in the beans and return to a boil. With the back of a large fork or spoon, mash about one quarter of the beans. Season to taste with salt and pepper.

Classic Alfredo Sauce

This ultrarich combination of butter, cream, and cheese has always been—and will always be—one of the truly great pasta sauces. Not only is it luscious, but it takes seconds to prepare, and the only cooking is melting the butter.

ENOUGH FOR 4 SERVINGS WHEN TOSSED
WITH 1 POUND PASTA

- **2 tablespoons butter**
- **½ cup heavy cream**
- **⅓ cup freshly grated Parmesan cheese**

Melt the butter in a large deep skillet over medium heat. When the pasta is cooked and drained, toss with the hot melted butter, the cream, and the cheese. Season with plenty of salt and pepper and serve at once.

Carbonara Sauce

In this classic, the hot fat from rendered bacon cooks the egg yolks into a thick and creamy sauce that is tossed with pasta and seasoned with the crumbled bacon and cheese. Be careful to add the hot drippings slowly to the yolks to keep them from scrambling.

ENOUGH FOR 4 SERVINGS WHEN TOSSED WITH 1 POUND PASTA

- **4 strips of bacon, finely chopped**
- **2 egg yolks**
- **½ cup freshly grated Parmesan cheese**

1 In a large skillet, cook the bacon over medium heat, stirring often, until crisp, about 5 minutes.

2 Meanwhile, in a pasta serving bowl, beat the egg yolks with a fork until blended. Remove the skillet from the heat and pour the hot fat and bacon bits slowly into the egg yolks, whisking constantly, until the yolks are thick and creamy.

3 Toss with hot cooked pasta and the Parmesan cheese. Season with salt and pepper to taste and serve at once.

Goat Cheese and Arugula Sauce

Arugula, also known as rocket, is a spicy, mildly bitter green leaf that looks a lot like the greens of radishes. Traditionally part of Mediterranean cooking, it is increasingly available on this side of the Atlantic, sold mostly as a salad green. Its piquant seasoning holds up well to pasta and is especially suited to the creamy musky quality of goat cheese.

ENOUGH FOR 4 SERVINGS WHEN TOSSED
WITH 1 POUND PASTA

- ¼ cup extra-virgin olive oil
- 2 bunches of arugula, washed and tough stems removed
- 1 small package (about 5 ounces) garlic and herb goat cheese, crumbled

1 In a large nonstick skillet, heat the olive oil over medium-high heat. Add the wet arugula and cook, stirring, until the greens wilt, about 2 minutes.

2 Stir in the goat cheese and season liberally with salt and pepper.

Gorgonzola and Walnut Sauce

Gorgonzola, the creamy mild blue cheese of northern Italy, is practically a sauce in itself. It melts luxuriously over hot noodles, and in this recipe is counterpointed by crisply toasted walnuts.

ENOUGH FOR 4 SERVINGS WHEN TOSSED WITH 1 POUND PASTA

- **2 teaspoons minced garlic in oil**
- **⅔ cup walnut pieces**
- **4 ounces Gorgonzola cheese, crumbled**

1 In a large nonstick skillet, toss the garlic in oil with the walnuts. Cook over medium-low heat, stirring constantly, until the walnuts are lightly toasted, about 3 minutes. Remove from the heat.

2 When tossing with hot cooked pasta, add ½ cup of the pasta cooking water and the Gorgonzola cheese. Season with salt and pepper to taste.

Bagna Romano

This sauce runs over with the complex salty fermented richness of oil-cured anchovies and garlic. It is a takeoff on the classic Roman dip, *bagna cauda,* enhanced with Romano cheese.

ENOUGH FOR 4 SERVINGS WHEN TOSSED WITH 1 POUND PASTA

- **1 small tin (2 ounces) flat anchovies in oil**
- **2 teaspoons minced garlic in oil**
- **¼ cup freshly grated Romano cheese**

1 Drain the anchovies, reserving the oil. Finely chop the anchovies.

2 In a small skillet, combine the garlic in oil with the anchovies and the oil from the anchovies. Cook over medium-low heat until you can smell the garlic strongly, about 1 minute. (The anchovies will practically dissolve.)

3 When tossing this mixture with hot cooked pasta, add ¼ cup of the pasta cooking water and the Romano cheese.

Asparagus, Garlic, and Cheese Sauce

This is a simple spring sauce that takes advantage of the first pencil-thin stalks of asparagus. The process is exceptionally easy. The asparagus are cooked with the pasta for the last minute. Then all you do is drain the two and toss them with some garlic in oil and freshly grated cheese.

ENOUGH FOR 4 SERVINGS WHEN TOSSED
WITH 1 POUND PASTA

- 1 pound thin asparagus spears, trimmed and cut into 2-inch lengths
- 1 teaspoon minced garlic in oil
- ½ cup freshly grated Parmesan and/or Romano cheese

1   Make this recipe when you are cooking the pasta. About 1 minute before your pasta is finished cooking, add the asparagus to the water. Drain the asparagus with the pasta, but do not shake off the water.

2   In a serving bowl, toss the asparagus and pasta with the garlic in oil and the cheese. Season to taste with salt and pepper.

Broccoli Rabe and Garlic Sauce

You either love broccoli rabe or you hate it. Decidedly bitter, it often takes a few tastes to get acclimated, but once that happens you will become a devoted fan. In this recipe, the rabe is simmered with an excess of garlic, for decidedly pungent results. Pass a bowl of grated Romano cheese on the side, if you like.

1 ½ CUPS, ENOUGH FOR 4 SERVINGS WHEN TOSSED WITH 1 POUND PASTA

- **1 bunch of broccoli rabe**
- **¼ cup extra-virgin olive oil**
- **3 cloves garlic, minced**

1 Trim off the tough ends of the broccoli rabe stems. Cut the broccoli rabe into 1½-inch lengths. Rinse well but do not dry.

2 Heat the olive oil in a large skillet over medium-high heat. Add the wet broccoli rabe, cover, and cook, stirring once or twice, until wilted, 4 to 5 minutes.

3 Stir in the garlic and ¼ teaspoon each salt and pepper. When tossing with hot cooked pasta, add ⅓ cup of the pasta cooking water.

Tomato and Basil Sauce

This uncooked recipe is the essence of garden freshness. Make it only when tomatoes are at their prime.

3 CUPS, ENOUGH FOR 4 SERVINGS WHEN TOSSED
WITH 1 POUND PASTA

- **3 large beefsteak tomatoes, cored and coarsely chopped**
- **¼ cup prepared basil pesto sauce**
- **2 cloves garlic, minced**

In the pasta serving bowl, toss the tomatoes, pesto, and garlic. Season with salt and pepper to taste.

Roasted Pepper, Artichoke, and Ricotta Salata Sauce

Marinated artichokes are one of the great convenience ingredients, providing us with one of the most sophisticated of vegetables in a form that cuts out more than an hour of cooking and scads of ingredients for seasoning and flavoring. If you prefer, you can use a jarred roasted red pepper here but, in that case, you'll probably need two, since they are small; skip to step 2.

1 1/4 CUPS, ENOUGH FOR 4 SERVINGS WHEN TOSSED WITH 1 POUND PASTA

- **1 large red bell pepper**
- **1 jar (6 ounces) marinated artichoke hearts**
- **7 ounces ricotta salata cheese**

1 Roast the pepper over a hot fire in a barbecue grill or under a broiler as close to the heat as possible, turning, until charred and blackened all over, 8 to 10 minutes. Enclose the pepper in a small paper bag and let steam 10 minutes. Rub off the blackened skin. Remove the stem, seeds, and ribs. Cut the roasted pepper into ½-inch dice.

2 Drain the artichoke hearts, reserving the marinated liquid in the jar. Chop the artichoke hearts. Mix with the reserved liquid, the pepper, and the cheese in the pasta serving bowl. Season to taste with salt and pepper.

Sun-Dried Tomato Pesto

Sun-dried tomatoes are used to full advantage in this easy uncooked pasta sauce. The tomatoes are pureed to disperse their intensity over a pound of pasta and helped along by some of the flavorful oil in which they are packed.

¹/₂ CUP, ENOUGH FOR 4 SERVINGS WHEN TOSSED
WITH 1 POUND PASTA

12 sun-dried tomato halves in oil plus 1 tablespoon of the oil

2 cloves garlic, crushed

24 basil leaves

1 In a food processor or blender, chop the dried tomatoes, their oil, the garlic, and basil to a coarse paste. Season to taste with salt and pepper.

2 When tossing with hot cooked pasta, add ½ cup of the pasta cooking water.

Tuna, Dill, and Garlic Sauce

If you don't like canned tuna, but you've only had it packed in water then you owe yourself a portion of this pasta. The tuna is moist and full flavored. The hazelnuts add a toasted richness that plays off a hefty dose of garlic and plenty of chopped fresh dill. Look for an Italian brand of tuna to find one packed in olive oil.

1 CUP, ENOUGH FOR 4 SERVINGS WHEN TOSSED WITH 1 POUND PASTA

- **2 cans (about 6 ounces each) tuna packed in olive oil**
- **3 cloves garlic, minced**
- **¼ cup chopped fresh dill**

1   Dump the tuna with its oil into a pasta serving bowl. Break the tuna into small pieces with a fork. Stir in the garlic, dill, a little salt, and plenty of pepper.

2   When tossing with hot cooked pasta, add ½ cup of the pasta cooking water.

Mussels in Red Sauce

Mussels are usually sold already cleaned, but you should still go through them carefully; discard any with open shells that won't close and scrub off any barnacles and seagrass that cling to the shells. Mussels should also be "debearded," which involves grasping any grassy goatees emerging from between the shells (these are used by mussels to anchor themselves in the ocean) and pulling sharply until the beard snaps off.

4 CUPS, ENOUGH FOR 4 SERVINGS WHEN TOSSED WITH 1 POUND PASTA

- **2 pounds cleaned mussels**
- **2 cans (14½ ounces each) Italian-style stewed tomatoes**
- **2 tablespoons extra-virgin olive oil**

1   Discard any open mussels that won't close. Place the remaining mussels in a large bowl, cover with cold water, and swirl in the water to remove surface dirt; drain. Cover the mussels with fresh water.

2   In a large nonreactive saucepan, bring the stewed tomatoes to a boil over medium-high heat. Drain the mussels and add them to the pan. Cover and cook, shaking the pan every minute, until all the mussels open, about 3 minutes. (Discard any that do not open.)

3   Toss the mussels with the oil and plenty of pepper. Season with salt to taste.

Sausage and Mushroom Sauce

This meat sauce is instantly flavored by the seasoning in the sausage. All you have to do is brown the meat, simmer the mushrooms, and add the tomatoes. The three ingredients provide everything else themselves.

3 CUPS, ENOUGH FOR 4 SERVINGS WHEN TOSSED WITH 1 POUND PASTA

½ pound hot Italian sausage, finely chopped

¼ pound mushrooms, cleaned and sliced

1 can (14½ ounces) diced tomatoes, juices reserved

1 In a large nonstick skillet, cook the sausage over medium heat until it loses its raw look, about 2 minutes, chopping and stirring to break up lumps and help the sausage cook through evenly.

2 Add the mushrooms. Continue cooking and stirring until the sausage begins to brown, about 3 minutes longer.

3 Add the tomatoes with their juices and season with salt and pepper to taste. Simmer for 5 minutes.

Savory Vegetables, Salads, and Sides

Rosemary Garlic New Potatoes

Mashed Potatoes with Celeriac

Buffalo Spuds

Great Garlic Galette

Breakfast Taters

Cumin Corn

Green Beans with Spiced Almonds

Creamed Herbed Spinach

Stir-Fried Broccoli Rabe

Broccoli with Toasted Walnuts

Asparagus with Smoked Salmon

Gingered Brussels Sprouts

Honey-Garlic Glazed Carrots

Apple Buttered Yams

Eat-It-Up Zucchini

Kale Smothered with Bacon and Onions

Wilted Chicory Salad

Southwest Tabbouleh

Roasted Pepper Rice Salad

Greek Spinach Salad

Basmati Rice with Pine Nuts

Fontina Polenta

Rosemary Garlic New Potatoes

True new potatoes are not just small, they're young. So young, that the sugars in the tuber have not yet been converted into starch. Lack of starch is why new potatoes do not need to be cooked as long as more mature specimens. Often small red potatoes are sold as "new," even if they have grown past that stage, but these impostors are easy to spot. Real new potatoes are never bigger than a golf ball, and they have a smooth, very thin skin.

4 TO 6 SERVINGS

1 large branch of fresh rosemary

12 ounces new potatoes, scrubbed

1 tablespoon minced garlic in oil

1   In a 10-inch microwave-safe baking dish, toss together the rosemary, potatoes, garlic, and ½ teaspoon each salt and pepper. Cover and microwave on high power for 5 to 6 minutes.

2   Stir, cover again, and microwave on high power for 5 to 6 minutes longer, until the centermost potatoes are tender.

NOTE   If you don't have a microwave these potatoes can be baked in a covered baking dish, adding a few spoonfuls of water, at 375°F for about 30 minutes.

Mashed Potatoes with Celeriac

Celeriac, or celery root, is likely to be the ugliest vegetable you are apt to encounter. Its gnarled muddy roots take considerable peeling, but once they're cleaned, they have amazing versatility. Raw, the texture of celeriac is firm, never hard, but when cooked it becomes quite creamy. The flavor is similar to that of a celery stalk with a pleasant sweet undercurrent.

4 SERVINGS

- **2 pounds russet potatoes (about 4), peeled and quartered**
- **1 pound celery root, peeled and cut into chunks**
- **⅓ cup light cream**

1 Place the potatoes and celery root in a large heavy saucepan. Cover with water and season liberally with salt and pepper. Cover and cook over medium-high heat until the water boils. Reduce the heat to medium and continue to boil until the vegetables are tender, about 20 minutes. Drain into a colander.

2 Mash the vegetables with a potato masher or a large fork. Mix in the cream. Season to taste with additional salt and pepper.

Buffalo Spuds

Roasted potatoes glazed with hot sauce and butter—it doesn't get any better. Serve with picnic food, such as barbecued or fried chicken, ribs, or burgers.

4 SERVINGS

- **2 pounds russet potatoes (about 4), scrubbed and dried**
- **2 tablespoons butter, melted**
- **2 tablespoons mild hot pepper sauce, such as Durkee Red Hot Sauce**

1   Preheat the oven to 425°F. Cut each potato lengthwise into 8 to 10 wedges.

2   In a large roasting pan, toss the potatoes with 1 tablespoon of the melted butter. Season to taste with salt. Roast for 1 hour, turning with a spatula every 20 minutes.

3   Meanwhile, heat the remaining butter and mix with the hot sauce. When the potatoes are done, toss with the spicy butter and serve.

Great Garlic Galette

Galette is French for a large, thin pancake. It can describe a crepe, tart, or large vegetable latke, as in this recipe. Because a galette is as big as the skillet in which it is cooked, the cake can be tricky to flip, but it's not hard and it's kind of fun.

4 SERVINGS

- **1 pound russet potatoes (about 2), scrubbed**
- **3 cloves garlic, minced**
- **¼ cup olive oil**

1 Grate the potatoes into a bowl of cold water. Mix until the water becomes cloudy. Drain, transfer to a large clean kitchen towel, and wring out as much water as possible. Toss the potatoes with the garlic and plenty of salt and pepper.

2 Heat 2 tablespoons of the oil in a large nonstick skillet over medium-high heat. Add the potatoes and press down into an even layer. Cover the pan and cook about 15 minutes, or until the potatoes are well browned on the bottom.

3 With the cover still on the pan, grasp the lid with a pot holder and flip the pan over so that the galette falls from the pan onto the lid. Remove the pan and return to the heat. Add the remaining oil to the pan and slide the galette, brown side up, back into the pan. Cook uncovered 10 minutes, or until the second side is brown. Slide onto a plate and serve cut into wedges.

Breakfast Taters

Whenever I bake potatoes, I always cook a few extra. It doesn't take any more time or energy, and the leftovers make the best hashed browns—much better than starting with raw shredded potatoes. Here the potatoes are browned with bacon to give them extra flavor. If you want to start with shredded raw potatoes you can do so, but you should remove the bacon once it is crisp to keep it from burning while the potatoes cook. The bacon can be returned to the mixture later.

4 SERVINGS

- **4 strips of bacon, chopped**
- **1 small onion, chopped**
- **4 baked potatoes, peeled and chopped**

1 In a large heavy skillet, cook the bacon over medium heat until crisp. Add the onion and cook until lightly browned, about 2 minutes.

2 Add the potatoes and season with salt and pepper. Chop and mix with a spatula to blend the bacon and onion with the potatoes. Pack down and cook until brown, about 5 minutes.

3 Cut into sections with the end of the spatula and flip. Keep browning, cutting, and flipping until the potatoes are heated through and speckled with lots of brown spots, about 8 minutes. Adjust the seasoning with more salt and pepper if needed.

Cumin Corn

Cumin is the aromatic spice in chili. Here it pairs beautifully with Mexican-style corn to make a tempting south of the border side dish.

4 SERVINGS

- **1 tablespoon lightly salted butter**
- **2 teaspoons ground cumin**
- **2 cans (11 ounces each) Mexican-style corn, drained**

1 In a medium saucepan, melt the butter over medium heat. Add the cumin and cook for 30 seconds, stirring constantly.

2 Add the corn and toss to combine. Heat through, stirring occasionally. Season to taste with salt and pepper.

Green Beans with Spiced Almonds

This tasty variation on green beans amandine profits from the powerhouse flavor of commercially prepared spiced almonds.

4 SERVINGS

1 pound green beans, ends trimmed

2 tablespoons butter

2 ounces spiced or Smokehouse almonds, coarsely chopped

1   Boil the green beans in a large pot of lightly salted water until barely tender and bright green, 3 to 4 minutes, depending on toughness. Drain and run under cold water to stop the cooking. Set aside.

2   Just before serving, melt the butter in a large skillet over moderate heat. Add the almonds and cook for 30 seconds, stirring frequently. Add the green beans and cook, tossing, until heated through, 2 to 3 minutes.

Creamed Herbed Spinach

Creamed spinach is usually a big deal, requiring a separate white sauce and a long list of ingredients. Here creaminess is instantaneous and lusciously unctuous, since it comes from a dollop of herbed cream cheese and a scattering of freshly grated Parmesan cheese.

4 SERVINGS

- 2 boxes (10 ounces each) frozen spinach or 2 bags (10 ounces each) cleaned fresh spinach
- ¼ cup soft garlic and herb cream cheese
- 1 tablespoon grated Parmesan cheese

1 The easiest way to cook spinach, either frozen or fresh, is in a microwave. If frozen, place the box right in the microwave and cook on high power for 5 minutes. If fresh, poke 2 holes in a bag of spinach and microwave on high power for 4 minutes. (If you don't have a microwave, cook fresh or frozen spinach in a large saucepan with about ½ inch water until soft. This will take about 8 minutes for frozen and 3 to 4 minutes for fresh.) When the spinach is cooked, drain in a strainer, pushing out as much water as possible.

2 Toss the hot spinach with the cream cheese and grated Parmesan. Season to taste with salt and pepper.

Stir-Fried Broccoli Rabe

Broccoli rabe is a leafy non-heading form of broccoli, but there the similarity ends. Rabe is an assertive vegetable, with a decidedly bitter afterglow. You either love it or hate it. If you like Belgian endive and radicchio, you will probably like broccoli rabe; you may even, like me, become an addict. Broccoli rabe makes a great accompaniment to grilled meats, especially lamb and duck. It is delicious served cold, heaped on a roll that's been dampened with olive oil and rubbed with garlic, and it's great tossed with pasta.

4 SERVINGS

2 pounds broccoli rabe

¼ cup extra-virgin olive oil

1 teaspoon finely minced garlic

1 Trim the broccoli rabe by cutting off the tough ends of the stems and any wilted leaves. Cut into 1- to 2-inch pieces and place in a large bowl of cold water. Swish back and forth to clean off any grit. Lift the broccoli rabe from the water and shake off the excess, but do not dry.

2 In a large heavy skillet or wok, heat 2 tablespoons of the olive oil over medium-high heat. Add the garlic, followed immediately by the wet broccoli rabe. It will mound out of the pan—don't worry. Just toss gently with the oil, and it will start to wilt. After about 1 minute, it should shrink enough to allow you to cover the pan. At this point add ⅓ cup water, cover the pan, and cook for 5 to 7 more minutes, until the stems are tender and most of the moisture has evaporated.

3 Drizzle the remaining olive oil over the broccoli rabe and season to taste with salt and pepper. Serve hot.

Broccoli with Toasted Walnuts

The cabbagey aspect of broccoli is enhanced by a rich crunch of toasted nuts. Walnut oil is used rather than butter to increase the nutty flavor. You can substitute olive oil for the walnut oil if you want.

4 SERVINGS

- **1 bunch of broccoli**
- **½ cup walnut pieces, chopped**
- **1 tablespoon walnut oil**

1 Bring a large pot of lightly salted water to a boil. Trim the ends from the stems of the broccoli. Peel the stems with a small knife. Slice the stems into ¼-inch-thick coins and the tops into bite-size florets.

2 Add the stems to the boiling water. Boil uncovered for 1 minute. Add the florets and boil 2 to 3 minutes longer until bright green and tender. Drain and transfer to a serving bowl.

3 Meanwhile, heat a large nonstick skillet over high heat until very hot. Turn the heat down to low, add the walnuts, and cook, stirring quickly, until the walnuts toast lightly, 1 to 2 minutes. Do not burn. Pour the toasted walnuts over the broccoli. Add the walnut oil and salt and pepper to taste, toss, and serve.

Asparagus with Smoked Salmon

The colors of this dish are spectacular, and its flavors are the flip side of the classic poached salmon and asparagus. Although it could accompany any light meat, poultry, or seafood, the vegetable is perfect served with an omelette or scrambled eggs.

4 SERVINGS

- **1 pound asparagus**
- **2 teaspoons extra-virgin olive oil**
- **1 ounce smoked salmon, cut into thin strips**

1   Trim the tough ends from the asparagus. Poach the asparagus in a skillet filled with simmering water just until bright green, about 2 minutes for thin to medium-thick asparagus.

2   Remove the asparagus with tongs and transfer to a platter. Drizzle on the olive oil and season with salt and pepper. Scatter the salmon over the top.

Gingered Brussels Sprouts

This method for preparing brussels sprouts is miraculous, transforming what has to be the country's most hated vegetable into a family favorite. Sweet, lightly crunchy, and pale springtime green, no one will suspect it is their nemesis. So don't let on.

4 SERVINGS

- **1 pint brussels sprouts**
- **3 tablespoons olive oil**
- **1 tablespoon finely grated or chopped fresh ginger**

1   Break off any wilted or yellowed leaves from the brussels sprouts. Slice the sprouts in half lengthwise. Place on their flat sides and cut into thin shreds, starting at the rounded ends.

2   In a large skillet, heat the olive oil over medium-high heat until smoking. Add the shredded brussels sprouts and the ginger and immediately toss. Stir-fry until the sprouts are lightly browned and tender, 3 to 5 minutes. Season to taste with salt and pepper and serve hot.

Honey-Garlic Glazed Carrots

The sweet and pungent combination of honey and garlic is striking in this recipe. The flavors mingle as they thicken into a syrup that cloaks the carrots. The process requires little attention until you near the end. Then, care must be taken to stir the syrup and watch the carrots carefully, since as the glaze reduces, its tendency to burn increases.

4 SERVINGS

- **1 pound carrots, peeled and cut into ¼-inch-thick diagonal slices**
- **1 tablespoon minced garlic in oil**
- **2 tablespoons honey**

1   In a large nonstick skillet, toss the carrots and minced garlic in oil over medium-high heat until thoroughly mixed. Add ¾ cup water and bring to a boil.

2   Add the honey and salt and pepper to taste. Simmer, stirring occasionally, until all but a thin film of honey glaze is left, 7 to 10 minutes.

Apple Buttered Yams

The sweet and spicy flavor of apple butter paired with garlic is all these sweet potatoes need. You'll never miss the brown sugar and butter you're probably used to.

4 SERVINGS

- **3 large yams or sweet potatoes (about 2 pounds), peeled**
- **1 teaspoon minced garlic in oil**
- **⅓ cup apple butter**

1 Cut the yams into small chunks. In a large heavy saucepan, toss the yams with the minced garlic. Add 3 cups water and salt and pepper to taste. Cover, bring to a boil, and reduce the heat to medium. Simmer for 15 minutes, checking occasionally to make sure the mixture doesn't boil dry. (Add more water, if necessary.)

2 Add the apple butter and cook uncovered another 10 minutes, stirring occasionally, until the yams are soft.

Eat-It-Up Zucchini

The success of this very easy recipe is dependent on quick cooking and on ridding the zucchini of its watery core of seeds. The fiber of summer squashes is delicate enough to soften in a few minutes, but the water released from the center section can take a quarter of an hour to get rid of. By just shredding the flesh and stopping before you get to the seeds, the problem disappears.

4 SERVINGS

- **2 pounds small zucchini (about 6), ends removed**
- **1 tablespoon minced garlic in oil**
- **½ teaspoon dried thyme leaves**

1   Shred the zucchini from top to bottom on the largest teeth of a grater. Do each side, stopping before you get to the seeds in the center. Discard the cores of seeds.

2   In a large nonstick skillet, toss the zucchini and minced garlic in oil over medium-high heat until throughly mixed. Add the thyme and cook just until the zucchini softens, about 2 minutes. Season to taste with salt and pepper.

Kale Smothered with Bacon and Onions

Kale is the oldest form of cabbage. Blue-gray-green, intensely curly, and provocatively pungent, it is strikingly beautiful and perfect with the strong flavors of smoked meat and caramelized onion. Kale is great served with a pot roast, a ham, or grilled tuna. It is also a highly nutritious green, rich in calcium, iron, and vitamin A.

4 SERVINGS

- **4 slices of bacon**
- **2 medium onions, thinly sliced**
- **1 pound kale leaves, stemmed and washed**

1   In a large deep skillet or Dutch oven, cook the bacon over medium heat until crisp, 4 to 5 minutes. Remove and crumble.

2   Add the onions to the bacon fat, reduce the heat to medium-low, and cook very slowly until golden brown, about 10 minutes.

3   Add the kale to the onions, along with any water still clinging to its leaves. Cover and cook over medium heat, stirring occasionally, until tender, about 10 minutes. Season with salt and pepper and serve.

Wilted Chicory Salad

The slightly bitter flavor and tough-crisp texture of endive-type lettuce is perfect for a warm dressing. The heat intensifies the flavors in the dressing, helping to tame the harshness of the greens. At the same time, the warmth softens the fibers of the vegetables creating a cacophony of contrasting sensations—soft and hard, sweet and tart, bitter and balmy.

4 ENTRÉE OR 8 SIDE-DISH SERVINGS

- **2 heads of escarole, chicory, or curly endive, cleaned and stemmed**
- **1 small red onion, peeled, halved, and thinly sliced**
- **1 cup red-wine-vinegar salad dressing**

1   Tear the escarole into bite-size pieces. In a large salad bowl, toss the escarole with the onion. Set aside.

2   In a small nonreactive saucepan, heat the dressing to boiling over medium-high heat. Pour over the salad, toss, and serve immediately.

Southwest Tabbouleh

This hearty grain salad crosses Middle Eastern tabbouleh with the spicy fresh vegetable flavors of Mexican salsa. Serve it with grilled seafood or chicken topped with Sauce Niçoise (page 150).

4 SERVINGS

- **1 cup fine-grain bulgur**
- **1 tablespoon extra-virgin olive oil**
- **1 cup chunky salsa**

1 In a mixing bowl, combine the bulgur with 1 cup cold water. Stir in the olive oil. Set aside to soak for 10 minutes, until all of the water has been absorbed.

2 Toss with the salsa. Season to taste with salt and pepper. Cover and refrigerate until chilled before serving.

Roasted Pepper Rice Salad

This salad is hearty enough to offer as a meatless entrée. Start with tomato soup and serve a green salad on the side.

6 TO 8 SERVINGS

2 cups brown and wild rice blend (see Note, page 129)

4 bell peppers of assorted colors

½ cup balsamic vinegar dressing

1   In a heavy saucepan, bring 4½ cups lightly salted water to a boil. Meanwhile, rinse the rice in several changes of cold water. Drain well. Stir into the boiling water. Return to a boil, then reduce the heat to a simmer. Cover and cook until all of the water has been absorbed, about 45 minutes.

2   While the rice is cooking, roast the peppers directly over a high flame or under a broiler as close to the heat as possible. Turn so that the skins of the peppers blacken evenly. When completely charred, place the peppers in a paper bag, close loosely, and set aside for 10 minutes. Peel the peppers with your fingers. The skin will slip off. If it clings to your fingers, rinse them and continue peeling, but avoid running the peppers under water, which will wash away much of their flavor. Remove the stems and seeds and dice the peppers finely.

3   When the rice is finished cooking, remove the pan from the heat, uncover, and drape a folded towel over the top. Replace the lid and allow the rice to rest for 10 minutes.

4 Toss the rice with the roasted peppers and the dressing. Season to taste with salt and pepper. Serve at room temperature or cover and refrigerate until serving.

NOTE I have used many brands of brown and wild rice blends, and though I do not normally recommend specific brands, I have found that Lundbergh rice blends are far superior to other more commonly available brands. Lundbergh rices can be found in most health food stores and in some supermarkets.

Greek Spinach Salad

Sometimes the most intense provocative flavor is surprisingly simple to achieve. Here it's all in the cheese.

4 ENTRÉE OR 8 SIDE-DISH SERVINGS

- **1½ to 2 pounds spinach, cleaned and stemmed**
- **6 ounces feta cheese, crumbled**
- **⅔ cup creamy garlic dressing**

Toss all the ingredients together in a large salad bowl and serve immediately.

Basmati Rice with Pine Nuts

Basmati rice is a fragrant long-grain rice from India. It cooks up into beautiful plump separate grains and has a natural subtle perfume that can make seasoning unnecessary. Both imported and domestic brands of basmati rice are sold in most markets. In this recipe, the rice is enriched and flavored with lightly browned pine nuts.

4 SERVINGS

- **1 cup basmati or other long-grain white rice**
- **2 tablespoons butter**
- **½ cup pine nuts**

1 In a heavy medium saucepan, combine the rice with 1¾ cups water, ½ teaspoon salt, and ⅛ teaspoon pepper. Bring to a boil over medium heat. Stir once. Reduce the heat as low as possible. Cover and simmer for 15 minutes, or until all of the water has been absorbed. When the rice is finished cooking, remove the pan from the heat, uncover, and drape a folded towel over the top. Replace the lid and allow the rice to rest for 10 minutes.

2 Just before serving the rice, melt the butter in a small skillet. Add the pine nuts and stir until lightly toasted, 1 to 2 minutes. Toss with the rice and season with salt and pepper. Serve warm.

Fontina Polenta

Polenta is the homiest of Italian starches. It is what mothers feed their children and remains one of the world's great comfort foods. It is quite simple to make, particularly in a microwave. This polenta is finished with fontina cheese. Do not confuse the brown-skinned Italian fontina with the red wax-covered Scandinavian cheese of the same name. Only the Italian type has the appropriate nutty flavor.

4 SERVINGS

- **1¼ cups yellow cornmeal**
- **4 ounces Italian fontina or gouda cheese, shredded**
- **1 tablespoon butter**

1 In a large, deep, heavy saucepan, whisk the cornmeal into 4 cups cold water. Season liberally with salt and bring to a boil over medium heat, stirring often with a long-handled wooden spoon. Reduce the heat to low and cook for about 20 minutes, stirring almost constantly, until the polenta is very thick and smooth. Beat in ½ cup more water and cook 5 minutes longer.

(Polenta can be made in the microwave. It won't take much less time, but it doesn't need to be tended as closely as stovetop polenta. Combine the cornmeal with 4½ cups water and salt to taste in an 8-cup microwave-safe dish or bowl. Microwave on high power for 7 minutes. Stir with a whisk until smooth, cover with a paper towel, and microwave on high power for another 7 to 8 minutes, until thick.)

2 When the polenta is done (regardless of cooking method), mix in the fontina and stir until melted uniformly throughout the polenta. Stir in the butter and season to taste with salt and pepper.

Sizzling Sauces, Marinades, and Rubs

Lemon Pepper Marinade

Provençal Elixir

Fajita Juice

Classic Barbecue Sauce

Barbecue Bath

Hot Pepper Teriyaki

Creamy White Wine and Garlic Sauce

Honey Mustard Glaze

Lemon Mint Marinade

Peachy Sweet and Sour Glaze

Hoisin Apple Glaze

Garlic Yogurt

Parmesan Crust

Brandied Pepper

Zesty Seasoning Rub

Santa Fe Rub

Sauce Niçoise

Old Bay Crunch

Real Steak Sauce

Smoked Chile Rub

Hot Pepper Honey

Holy Moley Mustard

Sauce Mignonette

Lemon Pepper Marinade

Lemon enhances flavor in the same way as salt, which is likely the secret behind the popularity of the lemon-pepper connection. This simple marinade is all-purpose, good for flavoring light meats, dark meats, fish, and vegetables with equal aplomb.

ABOUT ½ CUP, ENOUGH FOR 4 PORTIONS
WITH MEAT OR FISH

- **1 large lemon**
- **¼ cup extra-virgin olive oil**
- **2 tablespoons cracked black pepper**

1 Remove the zest from the lemon with a fine-tooth grater or a zester. If removed with a zester, chop finely.

2 Squeeze the juice from the lemon and combine with the zest, olive oil, and cracked pepper. Season to taste with salt. Use as a marinade for grilled chicken, ribs, fish, roasts, or chops.

Provençal Elixir

The heart of southern French cooking is simple—fruity olive oil and lots and lots of garlic. After that it can be enhanced with musky ripe olives, meaty anchovies, or the fragrant blend of herbs known as herbes de Provence. Although the blend can vary, it is most often a mixture of basil, fennel seed, lavender, marjoram, rosemary, sage, savory, and thyme. Herbes de Provence is sold along with other herb blends at your supermarket.

ABOUT ½ CUP, ENOUGH FOR 4 PORTIONS WITH MEAT OR FISH

- **½ cup extra-virgin olive oil**
- **1 tablespoon herbes de Provence**
- **2 teaspoons minced garlic**

1 Combine the olive oil and herbes de Provence in a small saucepan or a microwave-safe bowl. Heat over medium heat or microwave on high power for 1 minute.

2 Stir in the garlic and season with salt and pepper to taste. Let cool. Use as a marinade for grilled chicken, ribs, fish, roasts, or chops.

Barbecue Sauces

Barbecue sauces change geographically. Yankee barbecue (is that an oxymoron?) is all sweet and sour tomato with just a tinge of heat. Southern barbecue is sugar and spice, and the barbecue of the Southwest and Mexico is tart, salty, and peppery. The next four recipes run the gamut. Fajita Juice is a Mexican-style barbecue, fragrant with lime zest, sparked with lime juice, and incendiary with jalapeño peppers. Classic Barbecue Sauce is pure generic Yankee sweet and sour, and the easiest barbecue sauce ever mixed. Barbecue Bath is a thinner, tarter version of a classic sauce, and Hot Pepper Teriyaki is a melting pot of Asian barbecues, blending Japanese teriyaki sauce with Chinese chili paste and colonial Indian ginger preserves.

Fajita Juice

ABOUT ½ CUP, ENOUGH FOR 4 PORTIONS
WITH MEAT OR FISH

- **1 large lime**
- **½ cup pickled hot jalapeño slices, finely chopped, 2 tablespoons juices reserved**
- **2 tablespoons Worcestershire sauce**

1   Remove the zest from the lime with a fine-tooth grater or a zester. If removed with a zester, chop finely.

2   Squeeze the juice from the lime and combine with the zest, chopped jalapeños, reserved pickling juices from the peppers, and the Worcestershire sauce. Season to taste with salt. Use as a marinade for grilled chicken, ribs, fish, roasts, or chops.

Classic Barbecue Sauce

ABOUT ¹/₂ CUP, ENOUGH FOR 4 PORTIONS
WITH MEAT OR FISH

- **½ cup spicy ketchup**
- **1 tablespoon Worcestershire sauce**
- **1 tablespoon apple cider vinegar**

Mix together the ketchup, Worcestershire, and vinegar. Season to taste with salt and pepper. Use as a sauce for grilled chicken, ribs, fish, roasts, or chops.

Barbecue Bath

ABOUT ³/₄ CUP, ENOUGH FOR 4 PORTIONS
WITH MEAT OR FISH

- ¼ cup ketchup
- ½ cup Italian dressing
- 1 teaspoon hot pepper sauce

Mix together the ketchup, dressing, and hot sauce. Use as a marinade and sauce for grilled chicken, ribs, fish, roasts, or chops.

Hot Pepper Teriyaki

- ½ cup teriyaki sauce
- ¼ cup ginger preserves
- 1 teaspoon Chinese chili paste with garlic

Combine the teriyaki sauce, ginger preserves, and 2 tablespoons water. Mix in the chili paste. Season with salt and pepper to taste. Use as a marinade for grilled chicken, ribs, fish, roasts, or chops.

Creamy White Wine and Garlic Sauce

This light wine sauce is made from a reduction of dry wine and shallots, and thickened with softened seasoned cream cheese, in much the same way that one would make a classic beurre blanc.

ABOUT ²/₃ CUP, ENOUGH FOR 4 PORTIONS WITH MEAT OR FISH

- 2 shallots, finely chopped
- 1 cup dry white wine
- 6 ounces garlic and herb cream cheese

1 In a medium skillet, combine the shallots and wine. Season lightly with salt and pepper and boil over high heat until the wine is reduced to about ¼ cup.

2 Remove from the heat and mix in the cheese until smooth and melted. Use as a sauce with grilled chicken or turkey or grilled or poached fish.

Honey Mustard Glaze

Over the last decade, honey mustard has infiltrated our collective palate with a provocative combination that, like so many of our favorite flavor pairings, is a combustion of opposites—sweet and salty, tart and rich, searing and aromatic. It's great on almost anything except dessert.

ABOUT ²/₃ CUP, ENOUGH FOR 4 PORTIONS
WITH MEAT OR FISH

- **3 tablespoons honey**
- **6 tablespoons spicy brown mustard**
- **1 tablespoon Worcestershire sauce**

Mix the honey, mustard, and Worcestershire sauce together. Season with salt and pepper to taste. Use as a glaze for grilled chicken, ribs, fish, roasts, or chops.

Lemon Mint Marinade

The combination of lemon and mint is purely Middle Eastern. The lemon provides a fresh citrus perfume and a mild acid that encourage the flavor of the mint to permeate the marinating ingredients. And the addition of olive oil ensures that even the leanest ingredients will stay moist during cooking.

ABOUT ¹/₂ CUP, ENOUGH FOR 4 PORTIONS
WITH MEAT OR FISH

- **1 lemon**
- **2 tablespoons dried mint leaves**
- **¹/₃ cup extra-virgin olive oil**

1 Remove the zest from the lemon with a fine-tooth grater or a zester. If removed with a zester, chop finely.

2 Combine the lemon zest with the mint and rub into the surface of whatever meat, poultry, or fish you are using with this marinade. Season on all sides with salt and pepper and refrigerate for 15 minutes.

3 Squeeze the juice from the lemon over the mint-coated meat, poultry, or fish and douse with the olive oil. Marinate as long as desired. Use as a marinade for grilled chicken, fish, pork, or veal.

Peachy Sweet and Sour Glaze

This is the fruity version of a honey mustard glaze.

ABOUT ¹/₂ CUP, ENOUGH FOR 4 PORTIONS
WITH MEAT OR FISH

- ¼ cup peach preserves
- ⅓ cup honey mustard
- 3 tablespoons lemon juice

1   Place the preserves in a small saucepan or a microwave-safe bowl. Heat over medium heat or microwave on high power for 30 to 45 seconds, until completely melted.

2   Stir in the honey mustard and lemon juice. Season with salt and pepper to taste. Let cool. Use as a marinade for grilled chicken, ribs, fish, roasts, or chops.

Hoisin Apple Glaze

Hoisin sauce is one of the great premixed sauces of Chinese cuisine. Like soy sauce, it is made from fermented soy beans, but hoisin also contains spices and sugar. It is thicker than soy sauce and makes an excellent base for a barbecue sauce or seasoning paste.

ABOUT ¹/₂ CUP, ENOUGH FOR 4 PORTIONS
WITH MEAT OR FISH

- ¼ **cup hoisin sauce**
- ⅓ **cup frozen apple juice concentrate, thawed**
- **1 teaspoon Asian sesame oil**

Mix together the hoisin sauce, apple juice concentrate, and sesame oil. Season with salt and pepper to taste. Use as a glaze for grilled chicken, ribs, fish, roasts, or chops.

Garlic Yogurt

Yogurt is innately acidic, naturally thick, and creamy, even if it is fat-free. It has everything a marinade needs all on its own. This recipe ups the ante with a dose of garlic and the complex aroma of extra-virgin olive oil.

ABOUT ³/₄ CUP, ENOUGH FOR 4 PORTIONS
WITH MEAT OR FISH

- 2 cloves garlic, minced
- ¼ cup extra-virgin olive oil
- ½ cup plain yogurt (fat-free if you prefer)

Mix together the garlic, olive oil, and yogurt. Season with salt and plenty of pepper to taste. Use as a marinade or a glaze for grilled chicken, fish, and light meats.

Parmesan Crust

Dry grating cheese provides an effortless way to season breadings. But, because cheese is ruined by high heat, it is important to protect it under a coating of bread crumbs. This means dredging your chicken, fish, pork, or veal in the cheese first, after which it can be dipped in beaten egg and coated with dry crumbs.

ENOUGH FOR 4 PORTIONS WITH MEAT OR FISH

½ cup freshly grated Parmesan cheese

2 eggs, beaten

1 cup Italian-seasoned bread crumbs

1   Mix the cheese with ½ teaspoon each salt and pepper in a wide, shallow bowl or pie pan. Put the eggs and bread crumbs in their own separate bowls or pie pans.

2   Rinse whatever meat, poultry, or fish you are using under cold running water but do not dry. Roll in the cheese. Dip in the egg and dredge in the bread crumbs to coat completely. You might have to roll the meat, poultry, or fish in the bread crumbs twice to get a good coating. Place on a rack to dry for 10 minutes. Fry or bake.

Brandied Pepper

Cracked black pepper infused with brandy is the ultimate condiment for steak. It's also good with veal, lamb, and pork. Unlike many recipes for pepper steak that overpower the meat with two coats of pepper, I only gild one side. To my palate, it keeps the balance of aromatic pepper and good beef in perfect alignment.

ENOUGH FOR 4 PORTIONS WITH MEAT

- **2 tablespoons cracked black pepper**
- **4 teaspoons brandy**
- **2 tablespoons extra-virgin olive oil**

1   Mix the cracked pepper with the brandy and set aside for at least 20 minutes, but preferably overnight.

2   To use, rub both sides of the meat you are using with salt to taste. Press the brandied pepper into one side of the meat.

3   Grill or broil, starting with the side that has no pepper. Serve drizzled with the olive oil.

Zesty Seasoning Rub

This all-purpose seasoning can be mixed up in larger batches and stored at room temperature for months in a tightly sealed jar. Use it in pinches as a seasoning for roasts and stews, or dole it out by the spoonful as a barbecue rub.

ABOUT ¼ CUP, ENOUGH FOR 6 TO 8 PORTIONS WITH MEAT OR FISH

- 2 tablespoons lemon pepper
- 1 tablespoon garlic salt
- 1 tablespoon brown sugar

Mix together the lemon pepper, garlic salt, and brown sugar. Rub into the surface of steaks, chops, chicken breasts, or ribs. Refrigerate for 1 hour and broil, grill, or roast.

Santa Fe Rub

New Mexico chile powder (also called Chimayo and Molido) is a specialty item that can be found in spice stores. It is made from the New Mexico chiles, a domestic pepper that is slightly sweet, full-bodied, fruity, and medium-hot. You can make your own by grinding dry New Mexico or milder Anaheim chiles.

ABOUT ¹/₄ CUP, ENOUGH FOR 4 PORTIONS
WITH MEAT OR FISH

- **2 tablespoons New Mexico chile powder**
- **1 tablespoon ground cumin seed**
- **1 tablespoon ground coriander seed**

Mix together the chile powder, cumin, and coriander. Season with salt and plenty of pepper to taste. Use as a rub for grilled or baked chicken, fish, and red or light meats.

Sauce Niçoise

Use this sauce for baking chicken, pork chops, or fish. Because it is made completely from convenience foods, the Mediterranean flavors explode as soon as the elements are combined. The recipe calls for two products, black olive paste and pesto, that you will probably find only in a specialty store, although I have seen them in upscale supermarkets. They can also be mail ordered from Dean & DeLuca, 560 Broadway, New York, NY 10012 (212) 431-1691.

ABOUT 2 CUPS, ENOUGH FOR 4 PORTIONS
WITH MEAT OR FISH

- **1 can (14½ ounces) diced tomatoes**
- **4 teaspoons black olive paste**
- **2 tablespoons jarred basil pesto**

Mix together the diced tomatoes with their juices, olive paste, and pesto. Season with salt and pepper to taste.

Old Bay Crunch

Once again, the magic of Old Bay seasoning comes to the rescue. This is a great coating for "oven-fried" chicken, fish, or pork. The buttermilk helps to tenderize the meat and give it tang, the Old Bay is all the spice anyone could want, and the Grape-Nuts are deliciously crunchy. Because the coating will protect the food as it bakes, you can use skinless chicken without fear of it drying out.

ENOUGH FOR 4 PORTIONS WITH MEAT OR FISH

- **½ cup buttermilk**
- **1 tablespoon Old Bay seasoning**
- **1½ cups Grape-Nuts cereal**

1 In a medium bowl, mix the buttermilk with the Old Bay. Marinate chicken, fish, or pork in this mixture overnight in the refrigerator.

2 Grind the Grape-Nuts to a fine powder in a food processor or blender. Season liberally with salt and pepper.

3 Remove the chicken, fish, or pork from the marinade and dredge in the Grape-Nuts mixture to coat. Bake on a greased sheet pan in a 350°F oven until done.

Real Steak Sauce

This is particularly good with steak, but I like it with grilled or broiled chicken, as well.

¹/₃ CUP, ENOUGH FOR 4 SERVINGS
OF MEAT OR POULTRY

- **2 tablespoons butter**
- **1½ tablespoons spicy brown mustard**
- **2 tablespoons Worcestershire sauce**

Melt the butter in a small saucepan over medium heat. Remove from heat and mix in the mustard and Worcestershire sauce with a small whisk. Keep warm. Serve with grilled meat or poultry.

Smoked Chile Rub

Use this rub to infuse any food with the flavor of a hardwood fire. It is made from chipotle chiles, which are smoked jalapeños. They are available in specialty food shops and in Mexican food stores. Handle the chipotles carefully; their oils can be quite irritating.

ABOUT 1/4 CUP, ENOUGH FOR 4 PORTIONS
WITH MEAT OR FISH

- **2 to 3 dried chipotle chiles, stemmed and seeded**
- **1 tablespoon ground cumin seed**
- **1 tablespoon light brown sugar**

In a spice grinder or mini-chopper, grind the chipotles to a fine powder. Mix with the cumin and sugar. Season with salt and plenty of pepper to taste. Use as a rub for grilled or baked chicken, fish, and red or light meats.

Hot Pepper Honey

This is the most wonderful substance on earth—sweet, tangy, and hot at the same time. Its one drawback is that it loses all its flavor when it's heated. Therefore, if you use it to glaze grilled or roasted meat, brush it on at the end.

1/2 CUP, ENOUGH FOR 4 PORTIONS

- **6 tablespoons honey**
- **5 teaspoons mild hot pepper sauce, such as Durkee Red Hot or Crystal Hot Sauce**
- **1 teaspoon lime juice**

Mix together the honey, hot pepper sauce, and lime juice until smooth. Use as glaze for chicken or pork, or as a spread for corn-on-the-cob or corn bread.

Holy Moley Mustard

This unholy communion of honey mustard and horseradish zaps the palate with vibrating sensations. It is simultaneously hot, sweet, tart, and savory.

**5 TABLESPOONS, ENOUGH FOR 4 PORTIONS
WITH MEAT, POULTRY, OR FISH**

- **¼ cup spicy brown mustard**
- **2 teaspoons honey**
- **1 teaspoon prepared white horseradish**

Mix together the mustard, honey, and horseradish. Use as condiment or marinade for beef, chicken, fish, pork, or seafood.

Sauce Mignonette

This classic vinaigrette is traditionally served with raw oysters and clams, although I have taken to using it as a fat-free, all-purpose dip or marinade for seafood, chicken, pork, veal, or vegetables.

**ABOUT ¹/₂ CUP, ENOUGH FOR 4 PORTIONS
WITH MEAT, POULTRY, VEGETABLES, OR FISH**

- **2 medium shallots, minced**
- **1 teaspoon crushed hot red pepper**
- **½ cup red wine vinegar**

Mix together the shallots, hot pepper, and vinegar with 1 tablespoon water. Season with salt to taste.

Three Ingredients Great on the Grill

Grilled Chicken Breast in Caesar
  Marinade

Grilled Chicken Paillards

Jalapeño Honey Mustard Pork
  Chops

Blue Cheese Burgers

Peachy Mustard Baby Back Ribs

Creole Lamb Chops

Rosemary Grilled Shrimp

Tuna Burgers

Hot Pepper Teriyaki Fish

Trout Grilled with Bacon and
  Mint

Tea-Smoked Clams

Garlic Grilled Corn

Grilled Vidalia Onions
  Dijonnaise

Grilled Portobello Mushrooms

Grilled Asparagus Romano

Chili-Grilled Potato Chips

Grilled Asian Eggplant

Grilled Honey Corn Cakes

Barbecued Pound Cake

Grilled Chicken Breast in Caesar Marinade

Here the richness of the dressing helps to keep the skinless chicken breasts moist in the inferno of a high fire. The first step in this recipe is to pound the chicken breasts to an even thickness, which helps the meat grill evenly. To pound meat, place it between two sheets of plastic wrap and use a smooth-faced pounder or a rolling pin to gently flatten the thicker parts.

4 SERVINGS

- **4 skinless, boneless chicken breast halves, trimmed**
- **1 large clove garlic, split in half**
- **⅔ cup Caesar dressing**

1   Pound each piece of chicken breast to an even ½-inch thickness. Rub the chicken all over with the cut side of the garlic and season with salt and pepper. Pour one-third of the dressing into a pan large enough to hold the chicken in a single layer. Place the chicken in the pan and pour the remainder of the dressing over top. Add the garlic halves. Cover and refrigerate for at least 1 hour.

2   Light a hot fire in a barbecue grill. Remove the chicken from the dressing and grill 4 inches from the heat for 3 to 4 minutes per side, basting frequently with the dressing in the pan. Stop basting 1 to 2 minutes before you finish cooking. The chicken is done when it is uniformly browned and firm to the touch.

Grilled Chicken Paillards

A paillard is a boneless piece of meat that is pounded paper thin, so thin that it cooks through in a matter of seconds. In order for the chicken to brown before it is overcooked, it is important to have your fire as hot as possible.

4 SERVINGS

- **4 skinless, boneless chicken breast halves, trimmed**
- **3 tablespoons extra-virgin olive oil**
- **1 clove garlic, minced**

1 Coat the chicken breast halves with 2 tablespoons of the olive oil. Place between sheets of plastic wrap and pound with a smooth-sided meat pounder or a rolling pin to a uniform thickness of ⅛ inch.

2 Mix the garlic with the remaining oil and season lightly with salt and pepper. Set the garlic oil aside.

3 Light a hot fire in a barbecue grill. Remove the plastic from the chicken and grill the breasts as close to the hot fire as possible for 1 minute per side, until browned outside and cooked through with no trace of pink in the center. Serve drizzled with the reserved garlic oil.

Jalapeño Honey Mustard Pork Chops

This recipe calls for a relatively new product: jalapeño Tabasco sauce. It is made from mild green jalapeño peppers. Although it sounds spicier than good old red Tabasco, it is more aromatic and not nearly as biting. Here it is mixed with the sweet tang of honey mustard for a flavor that envelops the palate without scorching it.

4 SERVINGS

2 tablespoons honey mustard

2 teaspoons mild jalapeño Tabasco sauce

4 pork chops, ¾ inch thick

1   Mix the mustard with the jalapeño Tabasco sauce. Coat the chops with this mixture and set aside for 10 minutes.

2   Light a medium-hot fire in a barbecue grill. Grill the pork chops 4 inches from the heat for 3 minutes per side, until browned, firm, and just white in the center but still moist.

Blue Cheese Burgers

These burgers are infiltrated with bits of blue cheese in every bite. Water is also worked into the burgers to add moisture. Together, the two additions keep the burgers juicy and succulent, even when grilled to well done.

4 SERVINGS

- **1½ pounds ground chuck, round, sirloin, or any combination**
- **2 ounces crumbled blue cheese (about ½ cup)**
- **¼ cup blue cheese dressing**

1 With your hands, blend the ground beef with ¼ cup cold water and ¼ teaspoon each salt and pepper. Gently mix in the blue cheese. Form into 4 patties 1 to 1½ inches thick. Do not pack tightly.

2 Light a hot fire in a barbecue grill. Grill or broil the burgers 4 inches from the heat, turning, until browned outside and cooked to a desired degree of doneness: approximately 3 to 5 minutes per side for rare, 5 to 8 minutes per side for medium, and 10 minutes per side for well done.

3 Serve each burger topped with the dressing, on toasted buns, if desired.

Peachy Mustard Baby Back Ribs

Back ribs are the rack of bones left over from a boned pork loin, making it one of the choicest of all parts of the pig. Unlike spareribs, back ribs are tender enough to grill without marination, and because they do not need time to tenderize, they can be cooked through in minutes.

4 SERVINGS

½ cup horseradish mustard

¼ cup peach preserves

2 racks (about 4 pounds) baby back ribs

1 Mix together the mustard, peach preserves, and ¼ teaspoon each salt and pepper. Coat the ribs with half of this mixture and refrigerate at least 30 minutes.

2 Light a medium-hot fire in a barbecue grill. Grill 4 inches from the heat for about 5 minutes per side, turning the racks frequently and basting with more sauce after every turn. Watch the ribs carefully as they cook; the sweet sauce burns easily. Cut a piece of meat from the thicker end of a rack to test for doneness. When they are done, the meat will be tender, with no trace of pink.

3 Cut into individual ribs and serve.

Creole Lamb Chops

If you love grilled lamb but avoid it because of the price, lamb shoulder chops may be the answer. Tougher than pricier rib and loin chops, shoulder chops have great flavor, but they must be marinated before grilling. The sweet and sour character of French dressing provides all the tenderizing necessary, and when perked up with a dash of hot pepper sauce, the effect is as complex as any time-honored bayou recipe.

4 SERVINGS

1 cup French dressing

1 to 2 teaspoons hot pepper sauce

8 shoulder lamb chops, about ½ inch thick

1 Mix the dressing and the hot sauce. Pour one-third of it into a pan large enough to hold the chops in 2 layers. Place half the chops in the dressing and top with another third of the dressing. Place the remaining chops in the pan and top with the remaining dressing. Cover and refrigerate for at least 4 hours.

2 Light a medium-hot fire in a barbecue grill. Lift the chops from the marinade; reserve the marinade. Grill the chops 4 inches from the heat for 8 to 10 minutes per side, basting with marinade every 2 minutes until the last minute or 2 of cooking time.

Rosemary Grilled Shrimp

In this recipe fresh rosemary leaves flavor the marinade, and rosemary branches create a flavorful smoke that permeates the shrimp. The shrimp are left in their shells as they grill to help retain moisture and transmute a shrimpier flavor into the flesh. To clean the shrimp without removing the shells, slit the shells down their backs and remove the vein underneath, but not the shells. This will also leave a path through which the marinade can flavor the shrimp.

4 SERVINGS

1½ **pounds jumbo (16 to 20 count) shrimp**

6 **branches of fresh rosemary**

⅓ **cup garlic vinaigrette**

1 Slit the shells of the shrimp down their backs and clean out the sandy vein that lies just under the shell.

2 Chop the leaves from 1 branch of rosemary and mix with the dressing. Add the shrimp, toss, cover, and refrigerate for at least 1 hour.

3 Light a hot fire in a barbecue grill. Throw the rosemary branches directly on the hot coals. Grill the shrimp 4 inches from the fire for 1½ minutes per side, or until the shrimp are opaque throughout and firm. Remove the shrimp to a platter and serve hot.

Tuna Burgers

Finely chopped fresh tuna looks deceptively like ground beef. It needs no binder to form patties, and, just like ground meat, it can be grilled to rare, medium, or well done. The finished product, however, is decidedly nonbeefy. Lean and clean, it is the perfect burger for lapsed carnivores. Serve on toasted buns, if desired.

4 SERVINGS

- **1 pound fresh tuna steak, dark sections trimmed**
- **¼ teaspoon garlic powder**
- **2 tablespoons olive oil**

1 Finely chop the tuna. Mix with 1 tablespoon water, ¼ teaspoon salt, ⅛ teaspoon pepper, and the garlic powder. Form into 4 patties. Pack well and coat with oil.

2 Light a hot fire in a barbecue grill. Grill the tuna burgers 4 inches from the heat for 3 to 4 minutes per side for medium, until lightly browned on both sides, but still slightly pink in the center.

Hot Pepper Teriyaki Fish

Teriyaki is Japanese barbecue sauce. Just like American barbecue sauce, it juxtaposes sweet, salty, and tangy into a thick stick-to-the-ribs elixir, which is sold bottled in as many different formulas as there are grill jockeys. For this recipe, I use San-J or Kikkoman All-Purpose Teriyaki Sauce and mix it with a mild hot sauce, such as Durkee Red Hot or Crystal brand.

4 SERVINGS

- **2 tablespoons teriyaki sauce**
- **1 teaspoon hot pepper oil**
- **4 (5-ounce) firm-fleshed fish steaks, such as tuna, swordfish, shark, or salmon**

1   Mix together the teriyaki sauce and hot pepper oil. Brush a thin film over both sides of the fish steaks. Refrigerate the fish for at least 30 minutes.

2   Light a hot fire in a barbecue grill. Grill 4 inches from a high fire for 3 to 5 minutes per side, until cooked to the desired doneness, brushing with more teriyaki mixture before and after turning.

Trout Grilled with Bacon and Mint

The combination of freshwater fish, smoked meat, and sweet herbs embodies the essence of campfire cooking. The bacon crisps, exuding a steady stream of flavorful juices that continuously baste the outside of the fish, while inside, herbs, tucked into the center cavity, release their aroma into the flesh. I like to serve lemon wedges on the side, to squeeze over the cooked trout.

4 SERVINGS

- **4 cleaned 8-ounce brook trout**
- **8 small mint branches**
- **4 strips of bacon**

1 Season the trout inside and out with salt and pepper. Place 2 mint branches in the cavity of each fish. Close the fish and wrap a strip of bacon around each one.

2 Light a hot fire in a barbecue grill. Grill the trout 4 inches from the heat, turning, until the bacon is crisp and the fish flakes to the touch, about 4 to 6 minutes per side.

Tea-Smoked Clams

Tea leaves create a pungent, acrid smoke that is absorbed by the clams as they steam open right on the rack of a grill. You will need loose tea (the leaves in tea bags are too finely ground), which can be bought in tins in any specialty store and in many supermarkets. The tea is mixed with sugar to help it create more smoke.

4 SERVINGS

- **½ cup loose black tea leaves, such as English Breakfast, Earl Grey, or Lapsong Souchong**
- **⅓ cup sugar**
- **24 littleneck clams, scrubbed**

1   Light a hot fire in a barbecue grill. Mix the tea leaves with the sugar and sprinkle over several layers of aluminum foil. Place directly on the coals and drizzle with water. Place the rack over the fire and heat until the tea starts to smoke.

2   Place the clams on the rack and cover the grill. Smoke for 4 to 5 minutes, or until the clams have opened. (Discard any that do not open.) Serve at once.

Garlic Grilled Corn

Grilled corn develops a smoky aroma and a roasted patina. In this recipe the effect is enhanced by continually basting the corn with garlic butter, some of which can be reserved to spread on the corn at the table.

4 SERVINGS

- **3 tablespoons butter**
- **1 tablespoon minced garlic in oil**
- **4 ears corn on the cob, husked**

1 Light a medium fire in a barbecue grill. Melt the butter. Stir in the garlic in oil and salt and pepper to taste.

2 Brush one side of each ear of corn with the garlic butter and grill 4 inches from the heat until browned, 2 to 3 minutes. Brush with more of the butter mixture and turn. Keep buttering and turning until the corn is tender and lightly browned, about 5 to 6 minutes in all.

Grilled Vidalia Onions Dijonnaise

Although I know people bite into sweet Vidalia onions as though they were apples, I have never been tempted. They are, after all, onions, and to my taste, the most delicious onions for grilling. Here they are marinated in a vinaigrette dressing, caramelized on a grill, and napped with a tangy mustard sauce. Of course, if Vidalias are not in your market, any other large sweet onion can be substituted.

4 SERVINGS

- **2 large Vidalia onions, each cut into 4 thick slices**
- **¾ cup olive oil salad dressing**
- **2 tablespoons Dijon mustard**

1 Brush the onions with ¼ cup of the dressing. Set aside for 15 minutes.

2 Light a medium-hot fire in a barbecue grill. Brush the onion slices with a little more dressing and grill 4 inches from the heat for 3 to 4 minutes per side, brushing with more dressing before and after turning, until tender and golden brown.

3 Slowly pour the remaining dressing (there should be 6 to 7 table-spoons left) into the mustard, whisking constantly. Blend until smooth and slightly thickened. Pour this dressing over the grilled onions and serve immediately.

Grilled Portobello Mushrooms

Portobellos are the beefsteaks of mushrooms. I've seen them as large as ½ pound each. Slather them with oil, spike them with garlic, char their crowns over a bed of coals, and you have the best vegetarian argument for abandoning meat ever devised.

4 SERVINGS

6 to 8 tablespoons herb-flavored olive oil

1 teaspoon minced garlic

4 Portobello mushroom caps (about ½ pound)

1   Mix ¼ cup of the oil with the garlic and ¼ teaspoon each salt and pepper. Wipe the tops of the mushroom caps clean with a damp paper towel and brush the garlic oil over both sides. Set aside to marinate for 20 minutes.

2   Light a medium fire in a barbecue grill. Brush the mushrooms with some of the remaining herb-flavored oil and grill 4 inches from the heat for 2 to 3 minutes per side, turning 3 times and brushing with more oil at each turn.

Grilled Asparagus Romano

Asparagus gain flavor on the grill. Perhaps it is the slight dehydration that concentrates their natural juices, or the interplay of smoke and fresh greenery, but the results are addicting. The intensity of the grilled vegetable is offset with a garnish of freshly grated Romano cheese.

4 SERVINGS

1 pound medium-thick asparagus, trimmed

¼ cup extra-virgin olive oil

2 tablespoons freshly grated Romano cheese

1   Light a hot fire in a barbecue grill. Coat the asparagus with half the oil. Grill 4 inches from the heat for about 2 minutes per side, until bright green, just tender, and lightly browned.

2   With tongs, remove the asparagus to a platter. Season to taste with salt and pepper. Drizzle the remaining olive oil over the asparagus and sprinkle the Romano cheese over the top.

Chili-Grilled Potato Chips

Avoiding fried chips? Try these. To cut them easily, use a mandoline or a large sharp knife.

4 SERVINGS

1½ pounds russet potatoes (about 3), scrubbed

¼ cup olive oil

1 teaspoon chili powder

1 Light a hot fire in a barbecue grill. Without peeling the potatoes, slice them into very thin (⅛ inch or less) chips. Coat well with olive oil.

2 Grill, turning, for 3 to 4 minutes per side, until lightly browned. Remove with tongs to a bowl and toss with the chili powder and salt to taste.

Grilled Asian Eggplant

Asian eggplants are the small, narrow variety that are sold usually at the greengrocer or in Asian markets. They are sometimes hard to find, but the search is worth it. I buy them whenever I can and adjust my meal plans accordingly. They deliver all the sweet, meaty qualities one wants in an eggplant with none of its bitter disadvantages.

4 SERVINGS

¾ pound Asian eggplants (about 4)

2 teaspoons Asian sesame oil

1 tablespoon teriyaki sauce

1 Light a hot fire in a barbecue grill. Cut the stems from the eggplants and slice each lengthwise into 4 slices. Coat with 1 teaspoon of the sesame oil.

2 Grill the eggplants about 4 inches from the heat for about 3 minutes per side, until the slices are softened and browned.

3 Remove with tongs and toss in a serving bowl with the remaining sesame oil, the teriyaki sauce, and ¼ teaspoon pepper.

Grilled Honey Corn Cakes

These corn cakes are perfect for a quick breakfast or dessert. Breakfast on the grill? Why not? You'll never find a tastier toaster.

4 SERVINGS

- **5 tablespoons softened butter**
- **1 tablespoon honey**
- **8 corn toaster cakes or 8 slices of corn bread**

1 Light a medium-hot fire in a barbecue grill. Mix the butter with the honey until well blended. Brush half this mixture on both sides of the corn cakes or corn bread.

2 Grill the corn bread about 6 inches from the heat until lightly browned, about 1 minute per side. Serve with the remaining honey butter on the side.

Barbecued Pound Cake

Charcoal toasted pound cake is slathered here with sweet orange butter. Decadence doesn't get any more innocent.

4 SERVINGS

- **7 tablespoons butter, softened**
- **2 tablespoons orange marmalade**
- **8 slices pound cake**

1   Light a medium-hot fire in a barbecue grill. Mix 4 tablespoons of the butter with the marmalade until well blended. Set the orange butter aside.

2   Melt the remaining butter and brush it lightly over both sides of each slice of pound cake. Grill the pound cake 6 inches from the heat until it is lightly browned, about 1½ minutes per side. Serve with the orange butter.

Just-a-Minute Desserts

Chocolate Mousse Cupcakes

Chewy Coconut Macaroons

Amaretti

Caramel Crunch Shortbread

Dark Mocha Mousse

Honeyed White Chocolate
   Mousse

Chocolate Flan

Cinnamon-Raisin Bread Pudding

Lemon Melba Hasty Pudding

Fat-Free Apple Crisp

Biscotti Parfait

Peaches with Raspberry Sauce

Gilded Strawberries

Strawberries in Warm Rhubarb
   Sauce

Warm Lemon Blueberries over
   Melon

Orange Brandied Prunes

Grilled Bananas

Warm Vanilla Pear Puree

Tangy Maple Applesauce

Espresso Granita

Lychee Sorbet

Chocolate Mousse Cupcakes

You will not believe that three ingredients can create this much happiness in your mouth. Oozing with a melted chocolate middle, these cupcakes will appear to be raw when taken from the oven. Don't worry and don't bake them any longer. The chocolate puddle will set into a luscious mousse that drips with every bite.

12 SERVINGS

2 bars (7 ounces each) milk chocolate

6 eggs

¼ cup plus 2 tablespoons flour

1 Preheat the oven to 325°F. Put the chocolate in a large microwavable bowl and microwave on high power for 2 minutes, until shiny, then stir until melted; or melt in a double boiler over simmering water.

2 Stir the eggs and flour into the melted chocolate with a whisk or wooden spoon. Ladle into a 12-cup muffin tin lined with cupcake liners.

3 Bake for 15 minutes, until the sides of the cupcakes are set but the centers are still liquid. Cool in the pan for 5 to 10 minutes. The centers will set into a warm mousse. Peel off the cupcake papers carefully.

Chewy Coconut Macaroons

My friend Esther McMannus came up with the prototype for these macaroons. I have simply streamlined the ingredient list. They are chunky, chewy, and voluptuous. A word of warning about unpanning: macaroons always stick. To avoid breaking them, peel carefully from their foil backing after they have had a chance to firm for at least 15 minutes.

ABOUT 16 LARGE OR 30 SMALL COOKIES

- **1 pound (4 cups) sweetened shredded coconut**
- **1 can (14 ounces) sweetened condensed milk**
- **3 egg whites**

1 Preheat the oven to 350°F. Place the oven racks in the middle and lower third positions. Line one or two sheet pans with foil.

2 Mix the coconut with the condensed milk just until coated. Depending on the moistness of the coconut, you might not need to use the entire can of condensed milk.

3 In a separate bowl, beat the egg whites with a pinch of salt until foamy. Mix into the coconut. Using a small (1-ounce) or standard (2-ounce) ice cream scoop, mound the macaroon batter on the lined pans, about 1½ inches apart.

4 Bake for 20 minutes for small cookies, or 25 to 30 minutes for standard size, until the macaroons are golden brown on top and well browned on the bottom. If baking two sheets at a time, switch positions halfway through baking. Slide the foil with its cookies onto a cooling rack and let cool for 15 minutes. Peel the foil off the cookies and cool on the rack completely.

Amaretti

These beautiful little macaroons are an Italian favorite. They come out crisp at the edges and slightly chewy at their center. They will keep fresh for a week at room temperature.

ABOUT 20 COOKIES

- **1 roll (7 ounces or about ¾ cup) marzipan**
- **1 egg white**
- **⅓ cup confectioners' sugar**

1 Preheat the oven to 325°F. Place the oven racks in the middle and lower third positions. Line one or two sheet pans with foil or kitchen parchment.

2 Mix the marzipan and the egg white into a thick dough. Place the confectioners' sugar on a plate. Drop the batter by heaping teaspoons into the sugar. Roll into balls and place about 1 inch apart on the lined pans.

3 Bake for 18 minutes, or until golden brown. If baking two sheets at a time, switch them top to bottom halfway through baking. Slide the foil or parchment with its cookies onto a cooling rack and cool for 5 minutes. Peel the foil off the cookies and set on the rack to cool completely.

Caramel Crunch Shortbread

If crisp toffee candy were reincarnated as a cookie, it would taste like this.

12 LARGE COOKIES

- **1 stick (4 ounces) unsalted butter**
- **½ cup packed dark brown sugar**
- **1 cup plus 3 tablespoons cake flour**

1 Preheat the oven to 375°F. In a small saucepan, melt the butter over medium heat. Stir until the butter browns lightly, about 2 minutes. Remove from the heat and immediately stir in the brown sugar and flour. Add 1 teaspoon of water and mix into a firm, crumbly dough.

2 Scrape the dough into an 8-inch round cake pan and pat into a solid even layer. With a fork, make perforated lines in the top of the dough, dividing it into 12 even wedges.

3 Bake for 20 minutes. Cool in the pan on a rack for 15 minutes. Unmold and let cool completely. Cut into wedges along the perforated lines.

Dark Mocha Mousse

Easier than pudding and richer than cake, chocolate mousse is the original three-ingredient dessert. As with most mousses, the eggs in this preparation are raw. If you are unsure of the safety of your eggs, or avoid recipes that call for undercooked eggs, you will probably want to skip this recipe.

4 SERVINGS

4 ounces semisweet chocolate, coarsely chopped

4 eggs, separated

2 tablespoons coffee-flavored liqueur

1 Melt the chocolate in a bowl set over simmering water or in a microwave on high power for 1 minute. Cool for 1 minute. Beat the egg yolks and liqueur into the chocolate until smooth.

2 In a separate clean bowl, beat the egg whites with a pinch of salt until they form soft, full peaks. Mix one-third of the whites into the chocolate to loosen it. Fold the rest in carefully.

3 Cover and refrigerate in the bowl or spoon into individual molds first. Chill for at least 2 hours, until set.

Honeyed White Chocolate Mousse

Honey has the perfect blend of floral flavors to complement the sweet vanilla and fatty richness of white chocolate. Do not heat the white chocolate over a direct flame; it is apt to scorch.

4 SERVINGS

- ¼ cup honey
- 5 ounces white chocolate, finely chopped
- 1½ cups heavy cream, chilled

1 In a small saucepan on top of the stove or in a microwave-safe bowl in the microwave, heat the honey until it bubbles, about 1 minute. Remove from heat and stir in the white chocolate until it melts. Cool to room temperature.

2 In a medium bowl, beat the cream with a pinch of salt until it forms round, soft mounds. Fold the white chocolate into the whipped cream.

3 Cover and refrigerate in the bowl or spoon into individual molds first. Chill for at least 2 hours, until set.

Chocolate Flan

This is a miraculous recipe. As it bakes, the chocolate in the milk sinks to the bottom, which becomes the top once the flan is inverted for serving. The result is a shimmering milk chocolate discus, glazed in caramel and lacquered with dark chocolate.

8 SERVINGS

- **1 cup sugar**
- **1 quart chocolate milk**
- **4 eggs, lightly beaten**

1 Preheat the oven to 350°F. Heat the sugar in a heavy saucepan over medium-high heat. After 2 minutes, start stirring and continue stirring until the sugar melts into a pale golden caramel, about 2 minutes longer. Watch carefully to make sure it doesn't burn. Immediately pour the caramel into a 9-inch round baking dish. Carefully tilt the dish so that the caramel covers the bottom of the dish in a thin even sheet. Work quickly because the caramel will stop flowing if it cools. When the bottom of the dish is completely coated, set it aside.

2 Add the chocolate milk to the saucepan. Any caramel clinging to the pan will immediately solidify. Heat the milk to a simmer, stirring occasionally. Any solid caramel will melt into the milk. Stir the hot chocolate milk slowly into the eggs, mixing constantly. Pour the custard into the caramel-lined baking dish and set in a larger pan of water.

3 Bake for 1 hour, or until a knife inserted in the center comes out with just a speck of custard clinging to it. Cool on a cooling rack to room temperature and refrigerate for several hours until thoroughly chilled.

4 To serve, run a knife around the perimeter of the custard and cover with a large rimmed tray. Invert onto the tray. Shake lightly to release the custard. When the custard drops, lift off the dish, allowing the caramel sauce to run over the top of the flan and down onto the tray. Serve the flan in slices with a bit of sauce spooned on top.

Cinnamon-Raisin Bread Pudding

In these three basic ingredients are everything you need for a classic bread pudding. The raisin bread provides fruit, spice, and filling. The pudding adds sugar, flavor, and thickener. And the milk is the liquid.

12 SERVINGS

1 loaf (16 ounces) raisin-cinnamon-swirl bread, cut into 1-inch dice

6 cups milk

2 boxes (3 ounces each) cook-and-serve vanilla pudding

1   Preheat the oven to 350°F. In a 9½-by-13½-by-2-inch baking dish, toss the diced bread with 2 cups of the milk. Let stand for 10 minutes.

2   Meanwhile, in a separate bowl, mix the remaining milk with the pudding until smooth. Pour over the soaked bread and toss lightly.

3   Bake for 1 hour, or until browned and set almost all of the way into the middle. Remove from the oven and cool on a wire rack for at least 15 minutes before serving. Serve warm or chilled.

VARIATION   You can make a chocolate bread pudding following the same procedure by substituting a chocolate loaf cake for the bread, chocolate milk for the plain milk, and chocolate pudding for the vanilla.

Lemon Melba Hasty Pudding

Hasty puddings happen on their own. Whenever you put cake and a soft summer fruit together, the fruit will leak juice and the cake will absorb it. A disastrous effect if you are looking for pretty, but just what is wanted for a pudding. Here the juice from peaches saturates a raspberry coffee cake, which swells and thickens the softening fruit into a perfect pudding.

6 SERVINGS

½ pound raspberry-filled coffee cake

5 ripe peaches, peeled and cut into ½-inch wedges

¼ cup plus 2 tablespoons lemon preserves

1   Preheat the oven to 350°F. Cut the coffee cake into ½-inch slices and line the bottom of a 9-inch pie plate with the cake slices.

2   Mix the peaches thoroughly with ¼ cup of the preserves (I find it easiest to use my hands). Arrange them evenly over the surface of the cake. Dot the remaining preserves on top.

3   Bake in the oven for 50 minutes, until bubbly. Serve warm.

Fat-Free Apple Crisp

Apples are sweetened and seasoned with spicy apple butter and topped simply with Grape-Nuts cereal. As the crisp bakes, the juice from the apples softens the Grape-Nuts slightly, but not enough to make them lose their crunch. Top, if you like, with a scoop of vanilla ice cream or fat-free frozen yogurt.

6 SERVINGS

6 flavorful apples (such as winesap, Jonathan, or Granny Smith), peeled, cored, and thinly sliced

½ cup apple butter

2 cups Grape-Nuts cereal

1   Preheat the oven to 350°F. Toss the apples with the apple butter in a 9½-by-13½-by-2-inch baking pan. Scatter the cereal evenly over the surface.

2   Bake the crisp for 1 hour. Serve warm or at room temperature.

Biscotti Parfait

This dressed-up ice cream looks and tastes like an Italian frozen mousse. You can alter the flavor endlessly by using different cookies, liqueurs, and ice creams.

4 SERVINGS

- **8 almond biscotti**
- **¼ cup amaretto liqueur**
- **1½ pints dark chocolate or butter almond ice cream**

1 Break the biscotti into small pieces with a mallet or rolling pin. Place the biscotti bits in a bowl and drizzle on 2 tablespoons of the amaretto. Toss to moisten.

2 Layer the cookies and ice cream in parfait or wineglasses: make 3 layers of each, starting with the ice cream and sprinkling ½ teaspoon of amaretto over each layer of ice cream. Cover tightly and freeze until serving time.

Peaches with Raspberry Sauce

The ecstasy of peaches and raspberries has been around since Escoffier christened the pair "Melba" after Nellie Melba, the reigning star of the Paris opera. Nellie may be long gone, but the combo has kept its star status for nearly a century.

4 SERVINGS

- **1 package (10 ounces) frozen raspberries in light syrup, thawed**
- **2 tablespoons fruit liqueur, such as peach schnapps, framboise, or Triple Sec**
- **3 large ripe peaches, stemmed, pitted, and cut into thin wedges**

1 In a medium bowl, mix the raspberries with 2 tablespoons of their syrup and the liqueur.

2 To serve, divide the peaches among 4 dessert dishes and top with the raspberry sauce.

Gilded Strawberries

To my mind, this easy dessert is also one of the most elegant. Beautiful strawberries, lightly infused with orange liqueur, are awash in a cloud of tangy cream.

4 SERVINGS

- **1½ pints fresh strawberries**
- **3 tablespoons Grand Marnier or other orange liqueur**
- **⅓ cup crème fraîche or sour cream**

1 Rinse, dry, and hull the strawberries. Cut them into halves or quarters, depending on their size. In a medium bowl, toss the berries with the liqueur. Cover and refrigerate for at least 1 hour.

2 To serve, divide the strawberries among 4 dessert dishes. Pour any juices in the bowl over the berries. Top each serving with a large dollop of crème fraîche or sour cream.

Strawberries in Warm Rhubarb Sauce

I love strawberry rhubarb pie, but hate that the strawberries always get overcooked by the time the rhubarb has softened. This recipe fixes the problem by simmering the rhubarb with strawberry preserves, then ladling the warm sauce over freshly sliced strawberries. That way the heat of the sauce gently warms the berries without overcooking them.

4 TO 6 SERVINGS

- **1 pound rhubarb, thinly sliced**
- **1 jar (12 ounces) strawberry preserves**
- **1½ pints strawberries, hulled and sliced**

1 In a heavy nonreactive saucepan, combine the rhubarb, ¼ cup water, and the preserves. Cook over medium-high heat, stirring to dissolve the preserves until the rhubarb is very soft, about 4 minutes.

2 To serve, arrange the strawberry slices on dessert plates and top with the warm sauce.

Warm Lemon Blueberries over Melon

The interplay of warm sauce and chilled melon vibrates on the palate, and the crimson blue of cooked blueberries is stunning set against the pastel flesh of the honeydew.

4 TO 6 SERVINGS

- **¼ cup lemon preserves**
- **1 pint blueberries**
- **1 large orange- or green-fleshed honeydew melon, chilled, seeded, and cut into wedges**

1 In a nonreactive saucepan, heat the preserves with ¼ cup water over medium heat, stirring, until they melt, 1 to 2 minutes. Add the blueberries and toss to coat, cooking them for no more than 1 minute.

2 Place the melon wedges in dessert bowls and spoon a portion of the warm blueberries over each melon wedge.

Orange Brandied Prunes

Stewed brandied prunes infused with thin strips of orange zest are a standard at Paul Bocuse's restaurant outside of Lyon. Now you can have this three-ingredient rendition at home for a fraction of the cost. They taste incredibly good and are spectacular served over ice cream or a plain cake.

6 TO 8 SERVINGS

8 ounces pitted prunes

⅓ cup sweet orange marmalade

½ cup brandy

1   In a small saucepan, combine the prunes with ½ cup water. Cover and simmer over medium-low heat for 7 minutes.

2   Stir in the marmalade, add another 2 or 3 tablespoons of water if the mixture looks dry, and simmer, covered, for 5 to 7 minutes longer, until the prunes are tender.

3   Remove from the heat and stir in the brandy. Store in a glass jar overnight or up to 2 weeks before serving.

Grilled Bananas

Because bananas melt over the heat of the grill, they meld effortlessly with the butter and honey around them. Serve on their own or topped with ice cream for a warm banana split.

4 SERVINGS

- **4 peeled bananas**
- **4 teaspoons butter**
- **4 teaspoons honey**

1 Light a hot fire in a barbecue grill or preheat a broiler. Place each banana on an 8-inch piece of foil. Place 1 teaspoon butter and 1 teaspoon honey on top of each. Wrap the foil around each banana, sealing tightly.

2 Grill or broil for 5 minutes on a rack placed 4 inches from the heat. Serve in the foil or over ice cream, if desired.

Warm Vanilla Pear Puree

Similar to applesauce, but more delicate and more gently perfumed, this is a beautiful fruit dessert. I serve it with crisp chocolate cookies, cake, or chilled chocolate shavings.

6 SERVINGS

6 large pears (about ¾ pound total) peeled, cored, and diced

⅓ cup sugar

1 vanilla bean, split lengthwise

1　In a heavy saucepan, combine the pears with the sugar, 1½ cups water, the vanilla bean, and a pinch of salt. Heat until boiling, reduce to a simmer, and cook for 8 to 12 minutes, until the pears are tender.

2　With a slotted spoon, transfer the pears to a food processor or blender and puree until smooth. Boil the liquid in the saucepan until lightly thickened and reduced to about ¼ cup.

3　Remove the vanilla bean pieces and mix the reduced liquid into the pear puree. Serve warm.

Tangy Maple Applesauce

In this tantalizing fruit dessert, the rhubarb brightens the flavor of the apple with a much-needed tartness. Maple syrup provides sweetness and its inimitable aromatic taste. The result is similar to applesauce, but more interesting.

ABOUT 8 CUPS, ENOUGH FOR 8 TO 10 SERVINGS

- **2 pounds apples (preferably McIntosh), peeled, cored, and cut into eighths**
- **1 pound rhubarb (fresh or frozen), sliced**
- **6 tablespoons pure maple syrup**

In a large heavy saucepan, combine the apples and rhubarb with ¼ cup water. Cook over medium heat, stirring occasionally, until all of the fruit is soft. Blend in the maple syrup and simmer another minute.

Espresso Granita

Granita is the Italian name for ice. This one is very intense and is made with frozen coffee rather than with plain ice infused with coffee syrup. The lemon zest reproduces a hint of the lemon peel that is traditionally served with cups of espresso.

4 TO 6 SERVINGS

3 cups brewed or instant dark roasted coffee, preferably espresso

1 tablespoon finely grated lemon zest

¾ cup sugar

1 In a small saucepan, combine the coffee with the lemon zest and sugar. Stir until the sugar is fully moistened. Without stirring, bring the coffee to a boil. Remove from the heat and let cool completely.

2 When cool, pour into a shallow pan and freeze. In about 1 hour, ice crystals will begin to form around the edges of the pan. Stir them into the more liquid portions. Continue to freeze, stirring the frozen portions into the liquid every half hour, until the whole mixture is a firm slush. This will take about 3 hours. If it should freeze solid, break into small pieces and crush in a food processor or blender.

Lychee Sorbet

Fresh lychees are one of my favorite fruits, but they are only available for a few weeks in the summer. The rest of the year we must make do with the canned product. This sorbet is one of the only ways I know to give canned lychees the spark of fresh fruit. If you buy lychees in sweet syrup, you will need no additional sugar.

ABOUT 1 PINT, ENOUGH FOR 4 SERVINGS

- **1 can (20 ounces) pitted lychees in heavy syrup (see Note)**
- **¼ teaspoon wine vinegar (red, white, or rice)**
- **1 egg white**

1   Puree the lychees with their syrup in a food processor or blender until completely smooth. Pass through a strainer into a bowl to remove any solid pieces. Whisk in the vinegar and egg white until well blended. Cover and refrigerate until chilled, at least 2 hours.

2   Freeze in an ice cream freezer according to the manufacturer's directions. Store in the freezer for up to 2 days.

NOTE   Canned lychees are available in the Asian grocery section of many supermarkets or at any Asian market.

The Convenience Food Connection

Spicy Black Bean Soup

Shanghai Sauce

Sweet and Sour Tomato Sauce

Tangy Sweet and Sour Sauce

Sweet and Sour Cranberry Chicken

Holiday Roast Turkey with Cranberry Corn Bread Stuffing

Reduced-Fat Extra-Crispy Oven-Fried Chicken

Bubby Heinz's Brisket

Two-Soup Mushroom Pot Roast

Five-Minute Chili

Baked Fish Dijonnaise

Thai Peanut Shrimp

Thin Mint Ice Cream Cake

Instant Chocolate Layer Cake

Butterscotch Banana Bread Pudding

Spicy Black Bean Soup

This soup takes advantage of one of the greatest convenience foods to come out in the last decade. Powdered, seasoned cooked beans are sold as an easy bean dip or taco spread, but they're also great for making soup or thickening sauces without a speck of fat. Here they're turned into a heartwarming full-flavored soup in minutes.

4 SERVINGS

1 box (7 ounces) instant black beans

1 can (15½ ounces) black beans, drained and rinsed

1 cup chunky salsa, hot or medium

1 In a large saucepan, bring 4 cups water to a boil. Stir in the instant black beans and canned black beans. Bring to a simmer and cook over medium heat for 3 minutes, stirring often.

2 Stir in the salsa. Season to taste with salt and pepper. Serve hot.

Shanghai Sauce

Use this easy all-purpose Asian-style sauce as a glaze or dip for grilled or roasted chicken, duck, pork, or beef. You may find both dark- and light-colored plum sauce in the market. Either will work, although the dark variety is more pungent. The lighter one, which is served as a sweet condiment in Chinese restaurants, is also called duck sauce.

ABOUT 1 1/3 CUPS, ENOUGH FOR 4 SERVINGS
WITH POULTRY OR MEAT

- **1 cup plum or duck sauce**
- **¼ cup soy sauce**
- **2 tablespoons minced fresh ginger**

Mix together the plum sauce, soy sauce, and ginger. Use at once or cover and refrigerate for up to 2 weeks.

The Sweet and Sour Connection

Sweet and sour is the antithesis of togetherness. Rather than meshing into a new and improved flavor ("swour"?), the pair refuses to combine. Instead they vibrate— sweet/sour/sweet/sour/sweet/sour. As soon as we try to commit our palates to one of them, the other flavor appears, wiping its predecessor away. The effect boggles the taste buds.

Convenience products tend to be either sweet or sour, which can make them dull when alone, but gives them great potential for forming intriguing combinations. I have come up with three delicious examples. Each is a little different. Sweet and Sour Tomato Sauce is the most intense and the sweetest. Tangy Sweet and Sour Sauce is more savory. Both sauces are great to use as a glaze for baked chicken, roast turkey, roast pork, baked pork chops, spareribs, beef ribs, and meatballs. Sweet and Sour Cranberry Chicken centers around the innate sweet and sour potential of cranberries. It has the meat built into the recipe, but its sweet and sour components are equally good with turkey or pork.

Sweet and Sour Tomato Sauce

ABOUT 2¼ CUPS, ENOUGH FOR 4 SERVINGS
WITH MEAT, POULTRY, OR FISH

- **1 can (10¾ ounces) condensed tomato soup**
- **6 tablespoons grape jelly**
- **6 tablespoons frozen lemonade concentrate, thawed**

In a small nonreactive saucepan, warm the soup with the jelly over medium heat, stirring often, until the jelly melts. Stir in the lemonade.

Tangy Sweet and Sour Sauce

ABOUT 2 CUPS, ENOUGH FOR 4 SERVINGS
WITH MEAT, POULTRY, OR FISH

- **6 tablespoons apricot jelly**
- **1 cup French dressing**
- **1 package (1 ounce) dry onion soup mix**

In a small saucepan, melt the jelly over low heat, stirring often. Mix in the French dressing and the onion soup mix.

Sweet and Sour Cranberry Chicken

1 can (16 ounces) whole berry cranberry sauce

½ cup Italian dressing

4 pounds chicken pieces, rinsed and dried

Preheat the oven to 400°F. Mix the cranberry sauce with the dressing. Pour a third of the sauce into the bottom of a baking dish. Lay the chicken pieces in the sauce in a single layer. Pour the remaining sauce over top, and bake for 50 minutes, turning the chicken every 15 minutes.

Holiday Roast Turkey with Cranberry Corn Bread Stuffing

The stuffing is sweet and savory, and the glaze deliciously tangy. But even without its complex flavors, any recipe that can feed more than a dozen people in festive grandeur with only three ingredients deserves unending admiration.

15 SERVINGS

2 cans (16 ounces each) whole berry cranberry sauce

1 bag (14 ounces) corn bread stuffing mix

1 (12- to 14-pound) turkey, rinsed and dried

1 Preheat the oven to 325°F. In a nonreactive medium saucepan, bring 1½ cups water to a boil. Add 1 can of cranberry sauce and stir to combine. Pour over the stuffing in a large bowl and gently mix until all of the stuffing has been moistened. Season with salt and pepper to taste.

2 Remove the giblets from the turkey cavity. Season the walls of the cavity with salt and pepper. Lightly spoon in the stuffing. Any extra stuffing can be spooned into the neck cavity. Fold loose skin over the stuffing and tie the ends of the drumsticks together. Place the turkey on a rack in a large shallow roasting or baking pan. Insert a meat thermometer into the thickest part of the breast or thigh, making sure it does not touch any bone, and roast for 2 hours.

3 Spoon any fat from the surface of the pan drippings. Mix the remaining can of cranberry sauce into the drippings and spoon over the top of the turkey. Roast another 2 to 2½ hours, basting every 20 minutes, until the thermometer reads 170°F. Allow the turkey to rest for 10 minutes before carving.

4 Skim as much fat as possible from the surface of the cranberry pan drippings. Slice the turkey and serve with the stuffing and the cranberry drippings.

Reduced-Fat Extra-Crispy Oven-Fried Chicken

Here the flavor comes from the dressing, while the cereal delivers the crunch. And none of the ingredients has a problem with fat, so neither should you.

4 SERVINGS

- **4 pounds chicken parts, skinned**
- **1 cup reduced-fat French dressing**
- **3 cups Special K cereal**

1   In a mixing bowl, toss the chicken with the dressing. Cover and refrigerate from 1 to 24 hours.

2   Preheat the oven to 450°F. Pulverize the cereal with a rolling pin, blender, or food processor until finely ground. Pour onto a large plate, pie plate, or a sheet of wax paper.

3   Lift the chicken from its marinade and roll each piece in the cereal until well coated. You may have to do this several times to get a thorough coating. Place in a single layer in a nonstick, glass, or ceramic baking pan. Bake for 45 to 50 minutes, until brown and crisp.

Bubby Heinz's Brisket

This is how my mother made pot roast. The brisket gives the broth its meat flavor and the ketchup and onions do the rest. My mother was the *bubby*, but her recipe was pure corporate-America ingenuity.

6 TO 8 SERVINGS

- **2 to 3 pounds beef brisket**
- **1 bag (16 ounces) frozen diced onions**
- **2½ cups ketchup**

1 Rub the brisket all over with generous amounts of salt and pepper. Place the brisket, fat side-down, in a cold Dutch oven. Place over medium heat and cook until the fat from the brisket starts to melt. You will see it glazing the bottom of the pan. Lift the brisket to make sure it isn't sticking and raise the heat to medium-high. Cook, turning once, until the meat is browned on both sides, about 4 minutes per side.

2 Add the onions and stir gently until they begin to thaw. Add the ketchup and 2½ cups water. Bring to a simmer, reduce the heat to low, cover, and simmer until the meat is fork-tender, about 2 hours. If the gravy is still a bit thin, remove the brisket and boil to the desired thickness. Skim as much fat as possible from the surface of the gravy.

3 Slice the brisket thinly against the grain and serve with plenty of gravy ladled on top.

Two-Soup Mushroom Pot Roast

When my mother didn't make her pot roast with ketchup, she did it this way.

- **2 pounds beef pot roast**
- **1 can (10¾ ounces) condensed cream of mushroom soup**
- **1 envelope (1 ounce) dry onion soup mix**

1   Rub the meat lightly all over with salt and pepper. Place the meat fat side-down in a cold Dutch oven. Place over medium heat and cook until the fat starts to melt. You will see it glazing the bottom of the pan. Lift the meat to make sure it isn't sticking and raise the heat to medium-high. Cook, turning once, until the meat is browned on both sides, about 4 minutes per side.

2   Add the soup, 1½ cans water, and the onion soup mix. Stir to combine. Cover and simmer over low heat for 1½ hours, or until the meat is fork-tender.

3   Lightly skim any fat from the surface of the gravy. Slice the pot roast against the grain and hold in the gravy until serving time. This dish reheats well.

Five-Minute Chili

Chili beans are kidney beans that are seasoned with cumin, oregano, a little hot chili, and green pepper. They are a great time-saver for this spur-of-the-moment chili. Dress this up with the traditional accompaniments—tortilla chips, diced onion, shredded cheese, and sour cream—and no one will ever guess the convenience connection.

4 SERVINGS

- **1 pound ground beef**
- **1 can (about 15 ounces) chili beans**
- **½ cup salsa, hot or medium**

In a large nonstick skillet, cook the ground meat over medium-high heat, stirring often, until it loses its raw look, 4 to 5 minutes. Add the chili beans and the salsa and simmer for 2 minutes.

Baked Fish Dijonnaise

Any firm-fleshed fish, such as bluefish, swordfish, salmon, orange roughy, or catfish, can be baked to great advantage. The sauce here is made right in the baking pan, which takes advantage of the fish's juices, the richness of sour cream, and the explosion of flavor that Dijon mustard imparts.

4 SERVINGS

- **⅔ cup sour cream, reduced-fat if you prefer**
- **3 tablespoons Dijon mustard, at room temperature**
- **1½ pounds firm-fleshed fish fillets or steaks, skinned and boned**

1   Preheat the oven to 375°F. Mix the sour cream and mustard together. Set in a warm place to lose its chill.

2   Season the fish on both sides with salt and pepper. Place in a baking dish large enough to hold the pieces in a single layer. Bake for 12 to 15 minutes, until the thickest parts flake to gentle pressure. With a wide spatula, transfer the fish to a serving platter.

3   Add the sour cream and mustard to the drippings in the pan. Stir to blend well and warm a bit. Immediately pour over the fish and serve.

Thai Peanut Shrimp

Bottled peanut sauce hasn't yet proved itself to be quite as versatile as ketchup or salsa, but it's still the new kid on the shelf, so the verdict isn't in. However, this recipe, which became an instant classic in our house, has given it entrée into more than a few barbecue sauces, a couple of soups, and a favorite salad dressing. Not bad for a newcomer.

4 SERVINGS

- ¼ cup all-purpose Thai Peanut Stir-Fry and Dipping Sauce
- ¾ cup canned unsweetened coconut milk
- 1½ pounds jumbo (16 to 20 count) shrimp, shelled and deveined

In a large skillet, combine the peanut sauce and coconut milk. Bring to a simmer over medium-high heat. Add the shrimp and cook, turning as necessary to ensure even cooking, until firm, about 2 minutes.

Thin Mint Ice Cream Cake

Girl Scout cookies possess the rare ability to assuage the guilt of gluttony with a redemptive dose of Scout support. You can't buy too many, because every box casts a vote for the future. What is there to do but to throw another Do-Si-Do down the gullet? This ice cream cake does its duty by getting rid of a whole box of thin mints in a single recipe.

12 SERVINGS

- ½ gallon mint chocolate chip ice cream
- 1 package (10 ounces) Thin Mints Girl Scout Cookies
- 1½ cups chocolate sauce or chocolate syrup

1   Place 1 tablespoon of ice cream in the center of one of the cookies. Top with another cookie and another tablespoon of ice cream. Continue alternating cookies and ice cream until you have 5 cookies and 4 layers of ice cream in a stack. Place in the freezer. Make 5 more stacks in the same way.

2   You will have 10 cookies left over. Chop these coarsely; there will be about ¾ cup of chopped cookies. Set aside.

3   On a baking sheet, place the first frozen stack on its side, so that the length of the stack runs across the width of the tray. Arrange the remaining stacks in the same way down the length of the tray, making sure that the sides of each stack touch the others next to it. Spoon the remaining ice cream over the tops and sides of the cookie stacks, smoothing it as necessary with an icing spatula to make a rectangular dessert. Freeze until firm.

4 Cover the top of the cake with the chopped cookies and press lightly into the ice cream to help them adhere. Cover with plastic wrap and freeze several hours, until hard.

5 Remove from the refrigerator about 10 minutes before serving. Cut the dessert crosswise in slightly diagonal slices and serve with the chocolate syrup.

Instant Chocolate Layer Cake

A homemade cake with no baking? This is the fastest way I know to an impressive dessert. It can be made in less than 10 minutes, and it uses three ingredients that no home should ever be without.

8 SERVINGS

1 bag (12 ounces) semisweet chocolate chips

1 cup sour cream or reduced-fat sour cream

1 (15-ounce) plain butter loaf cake

1 Melt the chocolate chips in a bowl set over boiling water or in a microwave on high power for 45 seconds. Stir until smooth. Mix in the sour cream until well blended.

2 Using a long serrated knife, slice the cake horizontally into 4 even layers. Place the bottom layer on a serving plate. Spread ½ cup of the icing over the cake. Top with the remaining layers, covering each one but the last with ½ cup icing.

3 Frost the top and sides of the cake with the remaining icing.

Butterscotch Banana Bread Pudding

This is sinful glop. Cake, bananas, and pudding meld together into a caramelized, banana-cream, crunchy nut, pudgy butterscotch confection that looks just terrible and tastes just grand.

8 SERVINGS

1 loaf (15 to 16 ounces) banana-nut bread, cut into 1-inch dice

4 large ripe bananas, sliced

1 box (3.4 ounces) instant butterscotch pudding

1   In a mixing bowl, toss the diced banana-nut bread with 1 cup water until uniformly moistened.

2   In a food processor or blender, puree half the banana slices. Add the pudding mix and process until smooth and thick, about 1 minute.

3   In a 2- to 3-quart casserole, layer the soaked bread, remaining banana slices, and banana-butterscotch pudding, making 3 layers of each in that order. Cover tightly with plastic wrap and chill for up to 1 hour before serving.

Index

White chocolate mousse, honeyed, 183
White clam sauce, 90
White wine and garlic sauce, creamy,
 140
Wild mushrooms, beef stewed with, 64
Wilted chicory salad, 126
Wine, white, and garlic sauce, creamy,
 140

Yams, apple buttered, 123
Yogurt
 garlic, 145
 lemon honey dip, 3

Zesty seasoning rub, 148
Zucchini, eat-it-up, 124